HAL TROSKY

HAL TROSKY

A Baseball Biography

WILLIAM H. JOHNSON

McFarland & Company, Inc., Publishers
Jefferson, North Carolina

ISBN (print) 978-1-4766-6645-7
ISBN (ebook) 978-1-4766-2676-5

Library of Congress cataloguing data are available

British Library cataloguing data are available

Front cover: Cleveland Indians first baseman Hal Trosky
(*Cleveland Press* Collection, Michael Schwartz Library,
Cleveland State University)

Printed in the United States of America

*McFarland & Company, Inc., Publishers
Box 611, Jefferson, North Carolina 28640
www.mcfarlandpub.com*

To all my friends in baseball and in Iowa,
to my family, and to my wife, Chris

Table of Contents

Preface

Who was Hal Trosky? The answer depends on your perspective, on where you sit when you think about baseball's history. If you are an Iowan, you may know him better as the first major league batting star to emerge from the eastern part of the state in the twentieth century. Baseball has been played in organized form in eastern Iowa since at least 1867, and the region has hosted professional baseball since 1890; the 1891 Cedar Rapids Canaries, in fact, fielded a roster that included a future major league star, in pitcher and Cedar Rapids native Billy Hoffer, as well as the brilliant import John J. McGraw. Trosky, though, was the region's first home-grown slugging luminary of the 20th century.

He played first base for both the Indians and the Chicago White Sox in the 1930s and 1940s, his career reaching its apex in 1936 when he led the American League in runs batted in (162) and total bases (405). Despite his offensive dominance that season—and several others in which his batting was well above league average—he has been consigned to relative historical obscurity. That anonymity is possibly attributable to his having played at the same time as Jimmie Foxx, Hank Greenberg, and Lou Gehrig, three future Hall of Fame first basemen who held a virtual lock on first base on the American League All-Star teams of the mid–'30s.

To a Cleveland Indians fan during the Depression, Trosky was one of the unofficial faces of the franchise in the 1930s, playing on the same team as future Hall of Famers Bob Feller, Earl Averill and Lou Boudreau and notching some of the gaudiest power numbers in the history of the organization. Called up to the major leagues in late 1933 after two years in the minors, Trosky parlayed that brief September stint into a legitimate opportunity to compete for a roster spot the following season.

1

A young, fun-loving Trosky hamming it up for reporters in Cleveland. In spite of his size, almost everyone who knew him remembers the big Iowan's "goofy" side (Boston Public Library, Leslie Jones Collection).

He not only made the varsity that next year, but he did so with a flourish. In 1934, his first full season in the majors, Trosky set American League rookie records for home runs, with 35—a mark exceeded in the eight succeeding decades only by Mark McGwire, Wally Berger, Hall of Famer Frank Robinson, Al Rosen, and recent slugging stars Albert Pujols and Jose Abreu—and runs batted in, with 142. That latter mark has been surpassed only by the immortal Ted Williams and the less-often-remembered Walt Dropo. Tack on Trosky's batting average (.330), on-base percentage (.388), and slugging average (.598), and those 1934 numbers describe one of the greatest rookie seasons in the history of the game.

A scant two months into the campaign, he smacked three home runs in the second game of a doubleheader between the Indians and the Chicago White Sox at League Park in Cleveland. While the feat is more common today, 80 years later, at the time it was a portent of tremendous power and talent in the 21-year-old. When Trosky reached that plateau, it had been achieved only once before in Cleveland's major league history, and as of 2016, only two younger players—Al Kaline and Eddie Mathews—have duplicated the feat. In the middle of the second decade of the twenty-first century, Trosky still sits at or near the top of the list of the greatest Indians sluggers ever.

On the all-time Indians lists, his offensive prowess stands out in even greater relief. Trosky's 216 (of 228 total) homers rank fifth in Cleveland history, and he is still in the team's top ten in doubles, total bases, RBI, and extra-base hits. He also ranks fourth in career slugging average and ninth in batting average. Finally, his 405 total bases in 1936 remains the highest single-season mark in franchise history, a period spanning more than 110 years.

The era in which Trosky played bridged a relatively important swath of both American and baseball history. The players and the stadiums are often imagined today in the grayscale and sepia tones of black-and-white photography, since most of the existing images from those years were colorless. The reality, though, was that Trosky's career encompassed a dramatic and vivid epoch. He signed his first professional contract less than a year after the stock market crash in October 1929, and ultimately hung up his spikes in late 1946, one year after atomic bombs fell on Hiroshima and Nagasaki. During his playing days, the world suffered one of the most severe economic crises in recorded history and experienced the bloodiest war ever fought.

Within the confines of baseball, Trosky's career also bridged eras. He was connected by association to both the earliest days of the modern game and the version played into the 1970s. One of his closest teammates on the Indians, pitcher Mel Harder, surrendered Ty Cobb's final career home run back in 1928, and another, Willis Hudlin, had given up Babe Ruth's 500th a year before that. One of his managers, Oscar Vitt, had been a teammate of Cobb in the second decade of the century, and another manager, Walter Johnson, was one of the original inductees into the Baseball Hall of Fame in 1939 (elected in 1936). As a young player, Trosky competed against Ruth, Gehrig, Foxx, Gomez, Grove—the list goes on and on. By the time he retired, he'd played with future Hall of Fame members Sam Rice, Bob Feller, Lou Boudreau, and Earl Averill, and against the likes of Ted Williams, Joe DiMaggio, and Hank Greenberg.

Even after he withdrew from the diamond, Trosky remained active in Iowa baseball until his health began to fail in the mid–1970s. His son, Hal Junior, had even reached the majors with the White Sox in 1958. The only significant aspect of baseball in the 20th Century that eluded Trosky was that he retired a year before Jackie Robinson and Larry Doby broke the color barrier in their respective leagues. Trosky never competed in an in-season game against the former Negro leagues players, although by all accounts of his personality he would have relished the challenge.

Returning to the question "Who was Hal Trosky?" the answer is slightly different if you are from the tiny hamlet of Norway, Iowa, 15 miles west of Cedar Rapids. In that case, your answer might be that Trosky put your town on the figurative baseball map. His major league stardom brought attention and a degree of renown to the burg, but it also, unofficially, sealed his appointment as the progenitor of a legacy of baseball success that culminated in the otherwise obscure town producing four major league players. Those players, both Troskys, Bruce Kimm and Mike Boddicker, along with many more minor league and college stars, and a high school program that won 20 state baseball championships between 1965 and the school's closing in 1991, give Norway a degree of baseball acclaim shared by few other places.

In 2006, actor Sean Astin even made a movie about Norway High School's baseball legacy. *The Final Season* won no Oscars itself, but the team that was the subject of the film won the school's 20th state baseball championship in a 26-year stretch. For years Trosky was held up as an example of the art of the possible, proof that sometimes talent and hard work do get noticed, and that large-scale success is possible even in small places. In his later years, Trosky watched as his alma mater defeated just about every significant high school baseball team in Iowa in reaching a collective level of baseball excellence which few other cities, much less such a small town, could reasonably expect.

Who was Hal Trosky? He was a farmer, a husband, a father of four (including a second-generation baseball player and insurance salesman, a professional pilot, a proprietor of a hair salon in California, and a nurse), a baseball player, a scout, coach, and a devout Catholic. He was only the 17th player in American League history to reach the 200 career home run plateau, posted a lifetime batting average of .302 in over 5,000 at bats, and drove in 1,012 runs during an 11-year big league career. At the start of the 2017 baseball season, Trosky's .522 career slugging percentage place him in the top 60 on baseball's all-time list, and his 162 RBI in 1936 still represent the 19th-highest single season total in baseball history.

It is easy to play the "what if" game when it comes to Trosky. What if he hadn't been sidelined by the excruciating headaches that ultimately derailed his career? What if he'd been able to play more than the 11 seasons, some partial, that he did complete? What if he'd been a Yankee, with the associated order-of-magnitude increase in attention that still comes with wearing the pinstripes? What if he hadn't played first base in the same decade, in the same league, with Jimmie Foxx, Lou Gehrig, and Hank Greenberg? Of course, there are other "what ifs" that are fairly posed: What if he'd played in an integrated league? What if he'd played the predominantly night schedule of today? The hypothetical musings are almost endless, but they are fair to think about in the context of Trosky's life.

The Trosky story, as alluded to earlier, runs deeper into the culverts of American history than might be obvious at first blush. It would be easy to pigeon-hole Trosky into a template as "big, corn-fed Midwestern slugger makes good in baseball." That sort of stereotyping, though, all but consigns the actual story of his life and the lives of those he touched, the critical details that comprise his biographical mosaic, to the threshold of irrelevance.

My serious interest in the Hal Trosky story began in 1994. He was my wife's great-uncle, and after hearing enough tales about the man, I began to look into some of the stories about the player. It was a fortunate choice, as with the assistance of both the Cleveland Indians and the Chicago White Sox, I was able to establish communications with several of his former teammates and opponents, all of whom have since passed away. Those conversations and correspondence stimulated a long period of research, and this book is the result. Drawing on publicly available information, interviews in the mid–1990s with his few living teammates, a wide collection of newspaper accounts, and private family collections, I have tried to provide the most comprehensive examination of his life to date.

One note on the narrative: Every quotation attributed to Trosky has been referenced in the notes section. Most of these came directly from newspaper and magazine articles published at the time, which

I've treated as primary sources. Some of those articles, however, came from cut-out clippings in the scrapbooks and files of Trosky's niece, Susan Volz. As any well-intentioned eight-year old girl might have done, she collected articles about her uncle without concern about the sources of those pieces. As I tried to match some of those clippings with newspapers of the time, I discovered that the eastern Iowa floods of 2008 destroyed 12 years of *Cedar Rapids Gazette* archives, as well as those of smaller newspapers from surrounding communities. Neither the Iowa State Historical Society in Des Moines, the *Gazette*, nor local libraries have a set of newspapers for the 1930s. In those cases that articles contained information used to support the biography, and which are corroborated by other sources but have incomplete attribution, I have noted that they are drawn from the archives of Susan Volz.

Hal Trosky's baseball story is in part the tale of Eastern Iowa in the early and middle part of the 20th century. It is a story of farming, of love, of anger, of bitterly cold winters and glorious summers, of seemingly superhuman talent, and of the luck that brought it all together. It is in part a chronicle of the explosive changes in the world during his lifespan. It is also a story of baseball in Cleveland during the Great Depression, an era when the city was a booming logistical hub, a time well before the name became a punch line for late-night comedians. His career spanned the final decade before integration of America's national pastime, and his experiences as a farmer and ball player during World War II underscored just how serious were the potential outcomes of those years. During his time in Cleveland and Chicago, he was hailed as a savior and pilloried for failure, a condition that is often the lot of successful professional athletes in communities where sports are part of the fabric.

Trosky's story after baseball is about family and faith, about living as a normal man who was frequently elevated in the collective eyes of his surrounding community. It is the tale of a good man doing his best for the place he loved the most. In 1841, in his essay "History," Ralph Waldo Emerson wrote, "All history becomes subjective; in other words, there is properly no history; only biography." The goal of this narrative, then, is to explore not only a remarkable baseball career, albeit one cut too short, but the story of his world from the perspective of his life.

It is a story worth telling.

❖1❖

Baseball Beginnings

In 1883, what Rand-McNally later described on their maps as Czechoslovakia was then loosely referred to as Bohemia (and now is two countries: Czech Republic and Slovakia). The region featured a mixture of what today would be called German, Austrian, Slovak, and Hungarian cultures, and it was there, in the city of Konigraatz, that the Trojovsky family had lived for generations. That year, 19-year-old Magdalene Walters, daughter of Mr. and Mrs. Peter Walters, married 22-year-old Charles Trojovsky who, like many of his neighbors, had immigrated to the United States from Bohemia following the country's war with Prussia, lighting in eastern Iowa. Charles at first tried farming, but found his temperament better suited to the cobbling trade that he had learned as an apprentice growing up back in the old country.

Families throughout the American Midwest were often quite large, owing in equal parts to long, cold winters and to the devout strain of Catholicism which still thrives in the region, but Charles and Magdalene had only four children. John, their eldest, married Mary Siepman from nearby Blairstown, Iowa, in 1903 and they, in turn, also had four children, including daughters Annette and Esther, and sons Victor and Harold, who was born on November 11, 1912.

The Trojovskys moved to their 420-acre farm outside Norway, Iowa, in 1917, when young Harold was five years old. Each day, per the metronome of the seasons that set the cadence of farm life, the entire family arose before sunrise to complete their respective share of morning milking and farming chores. Even when the boy was old enough to attend St. Michael's Catholic Parochial school in town, he would return to the homestead just south of town each evening to his farming duties. He displayed no special academic gifts, and was largely an average student, but he was eventually one of the taller kids in any of his class or team pictures.

The John Trojovsky Family, ca: 1917. *Left to right*: Hal's sister Annette, father John, brother Victor (behind Hal), mother Mary and sister Esther (courtesy Susan Volz).

Trosky's Early Baseball Years

The youngest Trojovsky fully expected to continue to farm with his father upon completing grammar school in 1926. Baseball changed that. St. Michael's only provided education through eighth grade, which was considered the standard for most of the boys in the area since they generally took up the family farming business once school was out. Perhaps because the family farm had finally become economically sustainable, the Trojovskys were able to place a higher value on education for their youngest child. Harold stayed in school through 12th grade.

In 1927, though, Norway High School needed a catcher, and the youngest Trojovsky, now aged 15, was drafted into the job. He later recalled to *Cedar Rapids Gazette* writer Tait Cummins, "My older

1. *Baseball Beginnings*

brother and my sisters never had a chance to go to high school, and partly because my father was a baseball fan and because the high school thought I would be a good catcher, I got the chance. My first two years there I was a catcher, and in my third year I turned to pitching. Of course I did some pitching for independent teams on Sundays, picking up what I could."[1]

Norway High School was typical of the more rural schools in that it was tiny. Twenty was a huge graduating class, and as a result, Trosky was able to act in school plays, engage in sports, and participate in just about any activity his parents permitted. It was sport, however, that gave the boy a chance to excel. He was the tallest kid in his high school class, so basketball was inevitable, but he most enjoyed Norway's nine-month-a-year passion: baseball. And Trosky was a star.

His early athletic successes, along with the accomplishments of talented teammate Jerry Meredith, gathered enough attention that they were able to attract a scout from St. Louis to Norway. St. Louis' roster at the time was a veritable "who's who" of baseball lore. It included future Hall of Famers Grover Cleveland Alexander, Jesse Haines, and Rabbit Maranville, and a young future All-Star in Pepper Martin, and was wrapped in the fame that came with winning the National League pennant in 1928. The attention on Trosky was flattering to both him and the whole town of Norway, especially when the scout suggested the big pitcher try out with the Cardinals' class D minor league team in Danville, Illinois.

Norway's St. Michaels School photograph, 1924. Hal Trosky is standing in the back row, sixth from the right, amid older boys on both sides (courtesy Susan Volz).

9

The 1930 Norway High School home baseball game. Of interest is the absence of fencing, a scoreboard, or any sort of manicured infield. This was the fourth baseball diamond in the tiny hamlet of Norway, and served a variety of community purposes (courtesy Susan Volz).

Trosky's coach on the Norway town team was C. J. "Jeff" Pickart, like almost everyone in the area a farmer, and he had no concept of how to advise the boy regarding a future in baseball. There was one major league ballplayer in the region, the teenager knew, who might be able to offer some useful counsel, so he sought out Bing Miller in the nearby town of Vinton. Miller was, at the time, a key member of Connie Mack's powerhouse Philadelphia Athletics, a team which had just played in its second of three consecutive World Series, and he was eager to speak with the boy.

The appearance of an ivory hunter, a real baseball scout, was testament to the spread of Trosky's reputation. In the earliest days of professional baseball, as the game transitioned from being merely a gentleman's recreation and began to generate revenue for owners and players, the extent—or lack—of each team's informal interrelationships with locals in various parts of the country was the main barrier to scouting potential players. The minor leagues were in a continual struggle for stability and visibility, with towns—even ones the size of Cedar Rapids—often unable to guarantee attendance or sponsorship from one year to the next. Still, the minors did provide a sort of structured opportunity to evaluate players in actual, roughly standardized competitive environments. The challenge for the major leagues was determining which "can't miss" prospect truly was legitimate, and which should actually be labeled "can't hit."

Major league teams initiated formal alignment with specific minor league teams in 1919, and the practice wasn't widely adopted for decades. Most minor leagues and teams aggressively retained their independence until the 1930s, but all were certainly happy to sell player contracts to big league teams for the right price.

In the early 1900s, teams hired scouts who would follow up on tips

A rare photograph of Hal Trosky (left) and "Jerry" Meredith, hamming it up for the camera on the main street of Norway, Iowa. Meredith was a brilliant infielder, in the Marty Marion mold, and was preparing to sign a professional contract when a car crash permanently damaged his shoulder and derailed his big league dream (courtesy Susan Volz).

from their individual networks of bird dogs, a name given to those who followed players but weren't empowered to sign them. At that time, major league teams might have only two scouts, one for the east and one for the west. Billy Evans, general manager of the Cleveland Indians from 1927–1935, had a budget of only $50,000 for the entire annual scouting program.[2] Those budgets covered not only scouting for new talent, but also advance scouting, pre-trade scouting, and the like. On top of that, the Indians' budget for signing new players was also just

Connie Mack and John McGraw, two icons from baseball's past. Mack offered Trosky a contract to play for the Philadelphia Athletics, but it arrived in the mail three days after the boy had signed with Cleveland. McGraw was one of Cedar Rapids' earliest baseball stars, playing for the then-new minor league team in the early 1890s (Boston Public Library, Leslie Jones Collection).

$50,000. The net pressure on the scouts was that almost all of their potential players had to be signed, but for not much money.

At the time, 18-year-old Harold knew little about scouting or contracts or playing baseball for big money, certainly nothing beyond what he might have picked up from reading game accounts. Those anonymous scouts, similarly, did not really know how good Trosky might become. It was a proverbial crapshoot for both parties, with both absorbing some risk against an improbable—but potentially enormous—reward. It is no wonder Trosky needed some reliable advice from a player like Bing Miller.

Miller's story shared many essential elements with Trosky's. Just over 20 miles north of Norway and 10 miles west of Urbana, nestled along the Cedar River, is the town of Vinton, Iowa. Vinton, founded in 1849, is larger than tiny Norway, and has produced a few major league sons of which to boast as well. In addition to modern pitcher Cal Eldred, who hails from Urbana, two other major leaguers from the town were brothers Edmund ("Bing") and Ralph ("Lefty") Miller. Lefty's career was brief, as he pitched only one inning (three-up and three-down) of one September game for the 1921 Washington Senators. Bing, on the other hand, enjoyed a 16-year playing career—including two World Series championships—and lived a baseball life until his death at age 71.

Edmund John Miller was born on August 30, 1894, in Cedar Rapids, but the Miller family soon moved to a farm in the town of Cheney, between Urbana and Vinton.[3] He was the second of eight children born to Norman and Philomena Miller, both of French and German descent, who had migrated to Iowa from New York City. The Millers had three sons and five daughters: Eugene, Edmund, Ralph, Alvina, Norma, Matilda, Ida, and Mary. Eugene, Edmund and Ralph all played baseball from snowmelt until the following winter, in addition to farm work and attending the Polk Township school.

"Up until the age of 11, Miller was known as Ed to everyone,"[4] but it was Eugene who first dubbed young Edmund with the moniker "Bing." The name came from a character in a comic strip that ran in the local newspaper, the Vinton Eagle. The character's name, "George Washington Bings," was appended to Miller first as "Bings," but later simply "Bing."

Miller entered organized baseball as a 16-year-old when he joined the Vinton Cinders, a successful town team that played their games at the Benton County fairgrounds. By 1912 he was the pitcher in the (Bing) Miller–(Eugene) Miller battery, and performed well enough to attract the attention of local teams from both Cedar Rapids and Clinton. Upon turning 18 in 1914, he opted for the $80 monthly salary from Clinton (a $10 advantage over the Cedar Rapids offer), and joined the Central Association. Over the next three seasons with Clinton, Miller continued to improve as a pitcher, once running off a ten-game winning streak before hurting his right arm. His talents as a hitter, however, were so great that he was retained and converted to the outfield.

In his new position, and in an everyday slot in the lineup, he spent one more pre-war season in the minors, splitting time between Clinton and Peoria (Illinois). In 1917 he was called up to military service and spent a year in France with the U.S. Army in an artillery unit. After that tour he rejoined the Tigers organization, but he never entered an actual game for Detroit. Instead, the team sent him to the minors, to the Atlanta Crackers, and after 26 games with that team he was shipped to the Little Rock Travelers. In Arkansas, Bing played for Norman "Kid" Elberfeld. The team had finished in the cellar in 1915, but by 1920 they laid claim to the Southern League championship, when Miller hit .322 and led the squad with 19 homeruns.[5]

"Organized baseball" was a loose term in the first two decades of the century, and lack of oversight led to Miller being sold twice by the Travelers, to both the Washington Senators and the Pittsburgh Pirates. Kenesaw Mountain Landis, named baseball commissioner in November 1920, was forced to decide which team owned Miller's contractual rights; he eventually ruled in favor of the Senators. Miller made the Senators squad in 1921. He was an old rookie at 26, but hit .288 over 114 games during the campaign.

Despite his success, he was traded to the Philadelphia Athletics as part of a three-team deal that winter. Washington sent Miller and Jose Acosta to the Athletics, and Frank O'Rourke to Boston, while Philadelphia shipped Joe Dugan to the Red Sox. To complete the deal,

Vinton, Iowa's Edmund "Bing" Miller being tagged out by Washington Senators' catcher Muddy Ruel in a 1925 collision at home plate (Library of Congress Prints and Photographs Division).

14

Boston moved Roger Peckinpaugh to the Senators. Washington also sent $50,000 to Philly to complete the transaction.

In 1927, his second major league season, but at the age of 27, he hit a career-high 21 home runs (fourth in the American League) and slugged at a .551 clip. He finished fifth in the batting race (.336), sixth in total bases, and 15th in the Most Valuable Player voting.

Despite Miller's prowess at the plate, manager Connie Mack had an excess of talent in the outfield, and beginning in 1924 Miller started to see time at first base. In June 1926, the Athletics traded Miller to the St. Louis Browns for Baby Doll Jacobson. The change of scenery evidently reinvigorated Miller's bat, as he hit .331 for the rest of the 1926 season, and followed that with a .325 average in 1927. The Browns, being the Browns and thus historically hapless, were always on the prowl for a better deal.

Something. Anything.

No move was out of the question if it might improve St. Louis' position in the daily standings. In December 1927, Connie Mack rescued Miller from oblivion by sending Dolly Gray to the Browns in a straight-up trade. Miller played the 1928 season as a senior citizen, a 33-year old right fielder who still hit well enough to finish sixth in the AL batting race with a .329 average. In a category of more dubious distinction, he led the loop with eight hit by pitches. The team finished second that year, though, presaging the championship efforts of the next three seasons.

The Philadelphia Athletics dominated the American League in 1929, and Miller was a significant contributor. He logged a career high in base hits (184, including 16 triples) on the way to hitting .331, and stole 24 bases. He also posted a 28-game hitting streak and topped that by hitting .368 in the World Series against the Cubs in buttressing a 4–1 Athletics victory.

On October 14, in Game 5 at Shibe Park in front of President (and fellow Iowa native) and Mrs. Herbert Hoover, Bing Miller snatched a small but enduring spot in the lore of the game. The Cubs' Pat Malone had held the Athletics scoreless through eight and one-third innings of a masterful pitching performance, and the game was just over an hour and a half long at the start of the ninth. The Cubs led, 2–0, but Philadelphia nosed its way back to a tie with a Max Bishop single and a Mule Haas homerun. Malone maintained his composure and enticed

Mickey Cochrane to hit a ground ball for the second out. Sadly, though, the enduring and tragic mythology of the Cubs is built on real heartbreak. An Al Simmons double and an intentional pass to Jimmie Foxx brought Miller to the plate with the series on the line. He promptly smacked a double off the scoreboard, and the Athletics took the game, 3–2, and the Series, 4–1.

During the 1930 season, Miller led the team in games played, at-bats, and steals, and drove in 100 runs, the only 100-RBI year in his career. The team earned a third consecutive American League pennant in 1931 and nearly claimed a third straight World Series, falling to the St. Louis Cardinals in seven games. This marked the end of the glory days in Philadelphia, though, and by 1932 Connie Mack began changing the Athletics roster.

Doc Cramer, a rising talent in the Philadelphia outfield, forced Miller to take up the art of pinch-hitting. After 1932, Miller never had more than 197 plate appearances in a single season. On January 14, 1935, Miller was sold to the Boston Red Sox, and he led the loop with 13 pinch hits. Miller played in his last big-league game on September 5, 1936, and on September 28 the Red Sox named him to replace Al Schacht as a coach. Miller remained in Boston through the 1938 season, and then coached for the Tigers from 1938–1941.

After 1941, Miller moved along to the White Sox, managed by former Athletics teammate Jimmie Dykes, and remained with them through 1949. In 1950, Miller took the final job of his coaching career with Connie Mack and the Athletics, and stayed with the organization until 1954, after which the team moved to Kansas City.

Miller finished his career with a lifetime .311 batting average, earned two World Series rings with the Athletics while playing in a third Series, and coached in one with the Tigers in 1940. By 1966, he was a widower living in Wynnewood, Pennsylvania, a suburb of Philadelphia. On Friday, May 6, Miller made his way to old Shibe Park, renamed Connie Mack Stadium in 1954 but still the site of Miller's greatest playing successes, for a night contest between the hometown Phillies and the cross-state rival Pirates. The game lasted over three hours and covered 11 innings, and the hometown nine won, 8–7. Driving home that night, May 7, Miller was injured in a car crash and rushed to Presbyterian Hospital in Philadelphia. He died six hours later, at age 71, and is buried at Calvary Cemetery in West Conshohocken, Pennsylvania.[6]

Trosky Turns Professional

"I borrowed my Dad's car one day," Trosky later related to *Cleveland Plain Dealer* columnist Gordon Cobbledick, "and drove the 30 miles to Miller's home. He suggested I delay answering the [Cardinals'] letter."[7] Miller knew Trojovsky's (he didn't change his name until he signed his first contract) reputation as a player and advised the teenager to do nothing until Miller had a chance to inform Mr. Mack.

Trosky drove home quite content that afternoon in 1931. He pulled the old sedan up his dirt driveway and walked into the kitchen to find his father seated in the kitchen with Cleveland Indians scout, and Cedar Rapids native, Cyril C. "Cy" Slapnicka. Trosky later told Cobbledick, "I liked Slap, and after we talked baseball for a while he suggested I sign with him." Evidently, Slapnicka had been aware of the boy's prowess and local reputation, but hadn't felt any urgency in pursuing him until he got wind of the Athletics' and Cardinals' interest.[8] "Cleveland, Philadelphia, and Danville all looked alike to me," Trosky said, "and I simply signed with the first fellow who stuck an actual contract under my nose."[9]

At that time, the barn on the Trojovsky's family plot had only recently burned to the ground, along with some outer buildings, and had driven the family to the edge of bankruptcy.[10] John and Mary were never ones to walk around with open hands, but baseball gave the young man the chance to send some money home, even if only a relatively tiny amount. This was the Depression, after all, so anything was more than nothing.

The Indians' deal was better than the Cardinals' offer, Slapnicka explained, because St. Louis wanted Trojovsky to sign with an affiliated minor league team in their system, not with the major league organization. The Indians were offering a contract and, since they had a Class D affiliate in Cedar Rapids, a chance to play near home in case things didn't work out. Slapnicka had spent the preceding hours convincing the elder Trojovsky that his boy's interests were important to the Indians, and that the chance to play locally against Mississippi Valley League competition would be ideal for honing the young pitcher's skills. After almost no deliberation, he chose the Indians.

Hal Trosky was wooed and signed by a genuine legend of the scouting world. Cy Slapnicka was born Cyril Charles Slapnicka in 1886, in Cedar Rapids. The switch-hitting pitcher had enough talent to throw more than 70 major league innings over two seasons, with the Cubs in 1911 and the Pirates in 1918, but not enough skill to make a decent living at the game. He retired with a 1–6 record and a 4.30 earned run average in the Deadball Era. He wasn't a great hitter, either, notching just three hits in 23 official major league at-bats. As a scout, however, he was in a league all his own.

Slapnicka had been hired by Cleveland general manager Billy Evans, himself a prominent umpire in the early decades of the game and later elected to the Hall of Fame, as the only full-time scout for the team. In the 1920s, he spent most of his time in his home territory of Iowa, along with part of Illinois, in search of prospective talent. It was—and is—fertile baseball land, and Slapnicka made the most of his opportunities.

Two of the many pitchers he signed, Denny Galehouse and Thornton Lee, recalled "Slap" as a genuinely good man who was very nice to his players.[11] In Kevin Kerrane's seminal history of baseball scouting and scouts, *Dollar Sign on the Muscle*, Hugh Alexander offered a terrific, if not completely flattering, description of Slapnicka: "Slapnicka looked like a scholar. You know, maybe a college professor. He wore little horn-rimmed glasses and had thin hair. Kinda small fellow. He'd been a ball player, not a real good one, but he'd been a ball player and I guess he had a sixth sense about talent, and later on he taught me. He was—I hate to use the word—he was a little bit of a conniver."[12]

One of Slapnicka's favorite tactics was to sign a player without dating the contract. If the player—for whatever reason—failed to live up to expectations, the signing team could technically, and legally, release him with no other obligation (not even a train ticket home). Trosky was relatively immune to this sort of risk, since the Indians started him in Cedar Rapids, but it's certainly possible that he was playing with an illegitimate contract.

In 1931 Slapnicka signed Harold Trojovsky of Norway, Iowa, not because he loved the big pitcher, but largely because he heard that Bing Miller (and, thus, rival Connie Mack) was interested. Trojovsky's relative in Cedar Rapids had been pushing the prospect to Slapnicka for a year, but it was only the fear of losing the boy to the competition that finally piqued the scout's interest.

The Minors

A contract offer from Connie Mack and the Philadelphia Athletics arrived three days later. Trosky returned the unsigned document with a note explaining what had happened and apologizing for the inconvenience. He was genuinely touched when Mack took time to respond back with his best wishes for the player's future career.

He signed his first contract Harold Trojovsky, but from then on used the shorter Trosky (the pronunciation of which would early on be butchered as "Trotsky" by members of the press). The contraction was done at the suggestion of an in-law who correctly predicted that the shorter name would be easier for someone in the public eye, someone like a baseball professional.

That sort of name change was common in that time. The great Athletics slugger Al Simmons was born Aloys Szymanski, and Indians Hall of Fame pitcher Stan Coveleski was originally christened Stanislaw Kowalewski. Those ballplayers were like many of that era, second- or third-generation European immigrants. The Anglicization of their names was essential for both the convenience of sportswriters and to make the players more palatable to some of the game's more xenophobic fans. Hal's siblings eventually followed suit, each opting for the shorter "Trosky."

Trosky reported to the Class D Cedar Rapids Bunnies in March 1931, playing for a $65 monthly salary. Managed by a 38-year-old, 5'8" firecracker, Paul Speraw, who had appeared in one big league game as a third baseman with the St. Louis Browns in 1920, the "Buns" played a slate of teams from Keokuk, Moline, Waterloo, Burlington, Rock Island, Davenport, and Dubuque. The Mississippi Valley League did not survive the Depression, a fate shared by many of the other small minor leagues, but it did represent a first step on the road to Cleveland.

In a rare Sunday scrimmage, Hal Trosky made his professional baseball debut as a pitcher in the fourth inning. The *Cedar Rapids Gazette* account of the contest specifically cited a "snorting fastball that accounted for five strikeouts." Trosky pitched three innings and gave up four hits. He was also 1-for-1 at the plate in his first experiment in batting left-handed.

Trosky had been signed as a pitcher who had the odd habit of hitting cross-handed (right hand below the left) from the right side of the plate. From his earliest days swinging sticks at bottlecaps in the family barn, he had fallen into the habit of gripping the bat at the knob with his right hand, then tossing the rock or bottlecap with his left hand before swinging. His sisters, Annette and Esther, both played baseball, and had actually been Trosky's most reliable tutors as a youngster. They were both right-handed batters, so Hal had mimicked them from the start. He proved so adept with the style that he'd never changed to a more conventional approach throughout his scholastic career.

Slapnicka, in a visit to the Bunnies' park to check on his prospects, took player and manager aside, and after some discussion the three agreed that Trosky keep his grip but switch to a left-handed batting stance. The change was providential. Slapnicka was in the stands a few weeks later to check on his project, and was studying his scorecard during batting practice when he was suddenly startled by a sequence of sounds. The first was a remarkably crisp and powerful crack of Trosky's bat as it met a baseball; the second was an immediate thud as the same ball impacted the left field fence.

Tait Cummins later recorded: "Slap had looked up sufficiently fast after the first bang to note that the ball was on a line like a rifle bullet—only to the wrong field. Slap knew that a hitter who could hit a line drive to the opposite field with sufficient power to carry all the way to the fence simply had to be something special."[13] The very next day Slapnicka told the young player that he had no future as a pitcher. Speraw told the young player to go find a first baseman's glove and give the position as a try. Trosky complied, but for the next few weeks he impressed no one. His competitive debut at first base came on May 13, in the closing innings of an exhibition against a talented Negro travelling league team called Gilkerson's Union Giants.

He went hitless in two attempts. The experience, however, was Trosky's first brush with true greatness on the baseball diamond, as the Giants often barnstormed with a "major league" collection of baseball talent.

Black Baseball in Cedar Rapids

Since the early days of segregated baseball, even before any of the formal Negro leagues were created, teams of talented non-white ballplayers toured throughout the region. The non-white aspect was an ill-defined standard. Light-skinned Hispanics might, with a bit of a name change, pass muster to play in the white Major Leagues, while a dark complexion virtually assured a player that he'd be consigned to either the Negro American or National leagues, or to a barnstorming troupe. In every case, though, the caliber of baseball played in the non-white leagues was outstanding.

The earliest black teams in the Midwest formed in 1874. As baseball spread, the inventory of teams slowly grew as well, but black baseball did not take a firm hold in Chicago until the 1890s, when Julius Avendorph created "the Chicago Society Baseball League."[14] As an off-shoot, some enterprising owners chose to take a different path, to take the game to the people instead of the reverse. The Gilkerson Union Giants were a pure barnstorming club, the rough equivalent of a high-level minor league team today, and while not part of any formal league, they offered top-notch competition to any team willing to pay.

Robert Gilkerson, a former infielder, purchased the Union Giants in 1917 from W. S. Peters,[15] a founding father of Chicago's black baseball community. Gilkerson recruited the best veterans, from former stars on the downside to journeyman players who were no longer at the top of their game but were still able to fill out a competitive roster, and together they hit the road every summer. Like the Kansas City Monarchs a decade later, the Union Giants travelled throughout the Midwest, often entertaining the crowds with some baseball wizardry/comedy before and after games while earning a reputation for giving people their money's worth throughout.[16] Among the more notable Gilkerson alumni were Ted "Double Duty" Radcliffe, one of the greatest of the Negro leagues players, and Andy Cooper. As travelling teams went, the Union Giants were the best in the American heartland.

Iowa, in general, was perhaps as open-minded as any part of the United States with regard to race. Sure, there were plenty of overt bigots, and the entire country lived with the narrative that the status quo, in terms of race relations, was working well (at least from the Caucasian point of view), but the state has always been more accepting than many others. Bud Fowler, the first black professional baseball player, had played for Keokuk, but that was baseball-specific. Iowa's relative color-blindness was a matter of public record.

The opportunity for Cedar Rapids' minor league team to play

against Gilkerson's Union Giants was invaluable to young players on the Bunnies, as the level of talent was in some cases close to par with that of the white major leagues. The Giants' 1931 spring swing through Iowa started in early May in Muscatine. On May 8, the *Muscatine Journal* noted that "Gilkerson has the best club this year he has ever had on the road. He has added Andy Cooper, a pitcher formerly with the Kansas City Monarchs ... and "Steel Arm" Davis, formerly with the American Giants."[17]

The 1931 Giants brought a fairly potent lineup into Cedar Rapids. Bazz Smaulding, himself a former Monarch, had joined the team that year and served as the primary pitcher and reserve outfielder. "Steel Arm" Davis was not with the Union Giants for long, as he was splitting his time with the big league Chicago American Giants in 1931. Davis had earned his nickname due to his reputed ability to pitch both ends of a doubleheader (similar to Joe "Iron Man" McGinnity in the major leagues), but by this time he was relying on his slugging prowess more than his arm.

Andy Cooper, another Gilkerson pitcher, had led the Monarchs to a 1929 pennant after seven successful years with the Detroit Stars. He was with the Giants for a very brief stint in 1931, before returning to Kansas City, and it is unclear whether he appeared against Cedar Rapids that afternoon.[18] If so, he was one of the greatest Negro leagues pitchers ever to play in the town; he was inducted into the Hall of Fame in Cooperstown in 2006.

Gilkerson catcher Carrol Ray "Dink" Mothell was in his final year in organized, domestic barnstorming in 1931, and he was joined by outfielder, pitcher, and future umpire Hurley Allen McNair on the squad. From any perspective, this was the best team that Speraw's boys faced that season. That Trosky went 0-for-2 against them was to be expected.

Barnstorming baseball in Iowa continued through the 1940s, with the Kansas City Monarchs even making an appearance in Watkins, Iowa, to play the best of the Norway and Watkins town teams. It was the Monarchs, under the auspices of another Iowan, future Hall of Famer James Leslie Wilkinson, who brought night baseball to many of the outlying towns in the Midwest. The team jury-rigged some small light stands on the backs of trailers that they could drag from game to game, allowing the game to go on regardless of the hour of the day.

One of Trosky's nephews, Harold "Pinky" Primrose (who went on to coach Cedar Rapids Washington to a state baseball championship and is a member of the American Baseball Coaches Association Hall of Fame) played on that team and still gets a chuckle from the memory of playing against the Monarchs. "We played pretty well, and got up about three runs. Well, the clowning-around stopped, and Kansas City smacked five straight doubles and ended up beating us by four or five runs. They were putting on a show for the crowd in the stands, and letting us keep the score close, but once we went up by a few runs, they got serious."[19]

In 1949, as one of several examples of Negro baseball in Cedar Rapids, the Monarchs took on the barnstorming Indianapolis Clowns at Memorial Stadium. Indianapolis had one particularly notable player, George "Goose" Tatum, who achieved his lasting fame as a member of the Harlem Globetrotters basketball team.

Later that year, in late May, the Monarchs returned for a "regulation Negro American league baseball game" against the Philadelphia Stars. League slugging champ (after the tragic, premature death of Josh Gibson) and future Hall of Famer Willard Brown was but one of the distinguished players for Kansas City, having played briefly for the major league St. Louis Browns in 1947. Gene Collins and Gene Richardson played on those barnstorming Monarchs teams (the former also earning a tryout with the Yankees that year), as did Buck O'Neil, the future symbolic leader of the effort to acknowledge and praise the body of Negro leagues baseball in America. Philadelphia was led by James "Bus" Clarkson, a player good enough even at age 37 to earn a 14-game tryout with the Boston Braves in 1952.

The best Negro leagues players to reside in the Cedar River Valley were, without doubt, Art Pennington and Horace Garner, both of whom played in the Cedar Rapids Manufacturers-and-Jobbers League once their professional days ended. Each enjoyed careers that look wonderful in retrospect, but were no doubt psychologically draining at the time.

Garner played for the Indianapolis Clowns in the late 1940s through 1950, and signed with the Boston Braves in 1951. That year, in Eau Claire, he batted .359 and earned a promotion to Class B Evansville for 1952. The achievement was notable in that it earned him yet another promotion for 1953, this time to the Jacksonville (FL) Braves of the Class A South Atlantic League. It was in Jacksonville that he and teammates Felix Mantilla and a young slugging star named Henry Aaron, along with two other players on different teams, became the first black players in that regional bastion of racism. Together Aaron, Garner and Mantilla helped integrate the entire league, just six years after Jackie Robinson had done so for the Dodgers in Brooklyn.

Horace injured his knee in 1954 but managed to play a few more years before arriving in Iowa in 1958, where at age 34 he batted .313 as a regular outfielder for the Cedar Rapids Braves in the Class B Three-I League. Garner was a star in the M&J industrial league as well, but he was just a couple of years too old—as a black player—to get a legitimate shot at making the major leagues. Garner passed away in 1995, two weeks shy of his 72nd birthday

Art "Superman" Pennington took a slightly different route. He was born in Memphis, Tennessee, in 1923 but grew up a few hours away in Arkansas. In 1941, at the tender age of 17 and after only two years of minor league barnstorming, he signed a contract with the Chicago American Giants. He played for the Giants for four years alongside and against some of the great players of the Negro leagues, teaming with players like Cool Papa Bell, Artie Wilson, and Double Duty Radcliffe, and competing against Sam Jethroe and future Hall of Famers Satchel Paige and Hilton Smith, before moving on to the Mexican League for three seasons.

Pennington was, by any measure, an outstanding player. Twice selected to Negro League East-West All-Star Games, his lifetime batting average there was .336, and he hit .300 over three seasons in the Mexican League as well. In addition, he homered off both Dizzy Dean and Sal Maglie in All-Star exhibitions.[20]

In 1949 Pennington returned to the United States and discovered Iowa. He played the 1952 and part of the 1953 seasons with the Keokuk Kernels, and the rest of 1953 and 1954 with the Cedar Rapids Indians. He took his final shots with St. Petersburg (Florida State League) and Modesto (California League) before retiring and going to work for the railroad and Collins Radio. It was with Collins that he, and Horace Garner, added a few more layers to Iowa's baseball story in the M&J.

On the Move in the Minors

Six days after his futile encounter with high-level Negro baseball, Trosky finally started another game at first base and proceeded to log seven more at-bats without a hit. Shortly thereafter he was benched, and then sold to Dubuque.

With his new team, Trosky returned to the mound. In one game against Rock Island, he struck out 13 batters, with each hitter going down swinging. The pitcher was credited with only five "called" strikes the whole day. Despite his potential, 1931 was the final season in which Trosky would pitch.

From that point forward, he was exclusively a hitter. Trosky played 52 Mississippi Valley League games that summer as a converted first baseman and, in 162 at-bats, managed 49 hits (including three home runs) for a respectable .302 batting average. He followed that mark in 1932 by hitting .307 in 56 games for Burlington of the Mississippi Valley League, and then .331 after promotion to Quincy in the Class B Three-I League. His 15 home runs in 68 games with Quincy snagged the attention of executives in Cleveland, and in 1933 Trosky began the season as a $200-a-month player with the Toledo Mud Hens of the Double-A American Association, the minors' highest classification.

A new professional: Hal Trosky, posing a quasi-action shot in full Burlington Bees uniform at the Trosky family farm in 1932. That year Trosky moved from Class D Burlington through Class B Quincy and all the way up to Toledo in the American Association (courtesy Susan Volz).

The 1933 American Association season opened with Trosky as an outfielder who used his thunderous bat to compensate for his defensive deficiencies. Steve O'Neill, the old catcher for the Indians' 1920 World Series champions, managed Toledo that year and was delighted to be able to pencil Trosky's name into the daily lineup. O'Neill also began daily tutoring sessions for the slugger on the nuances of infield play, footwork, decision making, and the subtleties of positioning. The regimen of one-on-one teaching in the morning, followed by practical application of the lessons in the afternoon games, combined to turn the hitter into a passable first baseman by the end of the season.

Years later, Slapnicka summarized the conversion of young Hal Trosky to *Cleveland Plain Dealer* reporter Gordon Cobbledick:

> He was a pitcher when I saw him in a county fair ball game in Iowa, but after watching him at bat just once I didn't care whether he could break a pane of glass with his fastball. I had never seen such a raw kid take such a vicious natural swing with a bat as he did, and it wasn't a wild swing either. It was plain that, along with his power, he had a good eye. None of us knew where he could play, but we tried him in the outfield in 1932 and, when we saw that he didn't have the natural knack that would enable him to become a really good outfielder, we switched him to first base. He was terribly awkward in his first few games, but he soon got over it and now he's as good a first baseman as you could expect.[21]

In 132 games for Toledo that year, Trosky drove in 92 runs. Occasionally switch-hitting, he posted a .323 average for the campaign, which put him among the league leaders and effectively ameliorated most of his defensive lapses. His 33 homers put him in second place in the American Association race, trailing only mighty Joe Hauser of Minneapolis.

The home radio announcers even tried to label him with the nickname "Tarzan." Edgar Brands later discussed that in a small insert in *The Sporting News*. Trosky joined the WTMJ radio team during a broadcast one afternoon in Milwaukee and told the announcers, "Don't call me Tarzan—Ma don't like that name. Call me Hal." Evidently Mrs. Trosky had been dutifully listening to the radio account of one particular home run, but her son "got a letter from Ma ... and she writes that she likes the way you described my home run ... but asked me to drop the Tarzan stuff."[22]

Joe "Unser Choe" Hauser, Trosky's primary competition in the power statistics, was a prodigious slugger who twice hit over 60 home runs in single seasons in the minors, but who also benefitted from playing his home games in the bandbox ballpark used by the Minneapolis Millers. In mid–1933, the day that Trosky hit his 16th homer to move into third place in the Association home run race, John Holland held second place with 17 knocks. Hauser, on the same date, already had hit 49, and the next day he smacked his 50th.

Trosky played well, though, driving in 92 runs in 132 games, and a passage in the Toledo paper by columnist Dick Meade underscores that point (although the diction is somewhat dated):

> I cannot recall any other American association batter ever causing the enemy infield to be thrown out of line. Joe Hauser and Nick Cullop also club with terrific power, but most of their crash hits are long and high. Trosky smacks many whistling rollers right past transfixed infielders. If Hal were swinging regularly on the small park at Minneapolis I am sure he would be pretty close to Hauser's showy mark. Many a ball is caught on Trosky's close to the right barrier. Besides, Hal loses a lot of distant blows to center or in the right center corner.[23]

At the close of the Mud Hens' season, Cleveland called.

❖ 2 ❖

Welcome to Cleveland

Cleveland was home to one of the original eight of Ban Johnson's American League franchises, reborn like the phoenix with the creation of the new league in 1901. In the early decades of the twentieth century, the city itself was anything but the punch line it became in the 1970s. In those later years, the abutting Cuyahoga River actually did catch on fire. The dismal reputation of the city fostered famous jokes like: "What's the difference between Cleveland and the Titanic? Cleveland has a better orchestra." It became a poster city for the Rust Belt and for a time came to embody bleak hopelessness that not even Dostoyevsky could imagine. But it was not always so.

On the heels of the Civil War, Cleveland had used her strategic position on the southern shore of Lake Erie, and her embrace of the fabrics and steel industries, to become a truly national economic leader. The Erie Canal indirectly connected Cleveland with the eastern seaboard, and made the city a logistical nexus for the western reaches of the United States. Then there was one Mr. John D. Rockefeller, an ambitious man who led a small group that founded Standard Oil and who soon became first-among-equals as a titan of American industry. "Standard Oil made Cleveland the center of American petroleum production. As a result, the city saw benefits in the form of … economics and humanitarianism."[1] Rockefeller was one of the titans of industry that had such a hand in growing America into a global commercial power, and his throne was firmly planted in Cleveland. All recent perceptions to the contrary, Cleveland was—and, arguably, is—a vital American city.

Professional baseball had existed in town since 1869, inaugurated when the local Forest Citys travelled south to square off against Harry Wright's Cincinnati Red Stockings at the opposite end of the state.

That year, 1869, is widely acknowledged as the first season of professional baseball, since those very Reds became the first organization in the sport to pay all of their players. No longer a game played purely for local entertainment and municipal reputation, baseball entered an entirely new world that year. The state of Ohio was ground zero for the undertaking. That early iteration of the Forest Citys lasted only three years before folding in 1872, and Cleveland teams ebbed and flowed sporadically through professional baseball until 1889. In that year, the Cleveland Spiders jumped from the American Association to the National League, their governing body until the team was disbanded in 1899.

In 1901, with the birth of the American League, the Cleveland Blues (which became the Bronchos in 1902, the Naps in 1903, and finally the Indians in 1917) became home to several of the greatest players in the history of the game. Hall of Famers Larry "Nap" Lajoie, Tris Speaker, Cy Young, Joe Jackson, and Addie Joss all played in what is now referred to as the "Deadball Era," and each had a significant role in building the team's and the city's reputation. There were only 11 major league cities in existence at the time, and the fact that Cleveland was among the elect spoke eloquently about its status as a major American city.

The 1933 Cleveland Indians that Hal Trosky joined were a scant 13 years removed from winning their only World Series to that time. That fabled Cleveland season, 1920, and that team, managed by the "Grey Eagle" himself, Tris Speaker, had been instrumental in preserving the public face of baseball following the notorious 1919 "Black Sox" scandal which played out over the following year. Cleveland infielder Bill Wambsganss executed the only unassisted triple play in Series history in 1920, and a young Joe Sewell—himself a future Hall of Famer— was plucked from the minors to replace Ray Chapman, the only big leaguer ever killed by a pitched ball.

The intervening years of the otherwise "Roaring '20s" had been less kind to the city. With the exception of a couple of second-place marks, in 1921 and 1926, the Indians had struggled to finish in the first division. Between the "Murderers Row" Yankees and Connie Mack's 1929–1931 juggernaut Athletics, there had been little oxygen left for the Clevelands and the Detroits and the Bostons of the junior circuit. Those owners of the less successful teams were often satisfied simply to finish with a winning record. Connie Mack observed on more than one occasion, "It is more profitable for me to have a team that is in contention for most of the season, but finishes about fourth. A team like that will draw well enough during the first part of the season to show a profit for the year and you don't have to give the players raises when they don't win." In the case of Cleveland, the city enjoyed all of the economic benefit realized from its enormous stake in manufacturing, and had exploited its location on Lake Erie to become a commercial giant before the 1930 crash.[2] In 1933, as with most American communities, the city was clearly descending into an existential economic struggle, but Cleveland's woes were psychologically compounded by the baseball team's inability to return to the level of its glorious World Series championship.

The Indians had played most of their 1933 American League slate in a state of mild disarray. Although the team had a future Hall of Fame outfielder in Earl Averill—who led the team in virtually every offensive category—and some excellent pitching in Wes Ferrell, Mel Harder, and Willis Hudlin, along with a local phenom in Joe Vosmik, the Tribe was heading toward a sub-.500 record by year's end. On June 9, owner Alva Bradley announced that player-favorite manager Roger Peckinpaugh had been fired. The straw that ostensibly broke the camel's back was a 1–5 homestand versus St. Louis and Detroit, but the action was all but inevitable. The local pundits had waged a public campaign to convince Bradley to replace the manager with someone competent (i.e., someone of whom they, the beatwriters, approved) even though, at the time Peckinpaugh was sacked, the team had a winning record at 26–25.

The pundits, as is often the case, won.

Cleveland sportswriter Fred "Whitey" Lewis recounted in his 1949 book, *The Cleveland Indians*, that Bradley seemed to enjoy the limelight, and so added a dramatic pause in his speech to the writers after Peckinpaugh's firing before announcing to the gathered reporters that "The new manager, gentlemen, is Walter Johnson."

Cleveland general manager Billy Evans, at the insistence of Bradley and against his own baseball instincts, had talked the future Hall of Fame pitcher out of a farming retirement and into the dugout in Cleveland. The establishment of what have always been collectively known as "baseball people," those lifers who had no purpose outside the game and whose presence and judgment ensured that wrecklessness and impulse did not harm the game, evidently did not trust Johnson's ability to manage. Baseball men like Evans had legitimate concerns about Johnson's prospects based on the Big Train's record leading the Newark Bears of the International League. Cleveland writers, as Bradley suspected, were a simpler lot, more like trout that are easily fooled by shiny objects, and were completely entranced by the mere presence of the legend. The pressure on Bradley instantly abated as the press' collective inner-fanboy turned the writers into fawning sycophants. The tactical move had a short shelf life, but Bradley was determined to enjoy favorable press if only for a brief time.

Johnson took over a good-but-not-great team in 1933 and ultimately guided the Indians to a first division finish, albeit with a losing record (75–76). Some speculated that the Big Train was ineffective because he was simply impatient with players less gifted than he had been, but his immediate concern late in the 1933 season (after, of all teams, the Senators had sewn up the American League pennant) was to get a jump on 1934.

Any managerial failing on Johnson's part could not be linked to failure as a player on the baseball diamond. Called the "Big Train" due to a universally respected fastball and pinpoint control, he was the dominant pitcher in his time. From 1907–1927, he won 20 games a dozen times, including the ten consecutive years of 1910–1919. He tossed a record 110 shutouts and from 1921–1982 was the major league career strikeout leader, a mark he held longer than either Ruth or Aaron owned their respective home run crowns. A few years after his hiring as Cleveland's manager, in 1936, Johnson would join Babe Ruth, Ty Cobb, Honus Wagner and Christy Mathewson as members of the first class ever elected to the National Baseball Hall of Fame in Cooperstown.

Willis Hudlin later observed that, while Walter Johnson was a great man, he had a tough row to hoe in Cleveland. "I never heard him use a cuss word," but he "didn't have too many horses to work with."[3] Still, after Averill, Bill Cissell, and Willie Kamm, and with pitchers Hudlin, Wes Ferrell, Oral Hildebrand, and Mel Harder in the rotation, the Tribe's foundation was reasonably solid. Johnson did have a problem at first base, though, since he was forced to rely on the slick-fielding but weak-hitting incumbent, utility man Harley Boss.

Boss had debuted with the Washington Senators in 1928 at the age of 19, and in 12 games had managed only three hits. He spent the next two years bouncing between Washington and the minors before being traded to the Indians in exchange for Bruce Connatser and Jack Russell. By the time Trosky showed up, Boss was batting .270, but had only one home run and 53 RBI in over 400 at-bats. He was a figurative donut hole in the Tribe's lineup.

Trosky's season with Toledo ended on Sunday, September 10, in Columbus, Ohio, and on Monday afternoon, September 11, 1933, 20-year-old Trosky started at first in place of Boss for the Indians in Cleveland. At the time, he was the fourth-youngest player in the American League, behind Frankie Hayes, Cecil Travis, and the Red Sox' Mel Almada. Trosky later recalled,

> I walked into the clubhouse and the manager said I'd play first base and hit fourth. When the regulars started taking batting practice, I waited my turn and stepped up to the plate. Billy Cissell, the second baseman, threw me out of the cage and yelled "Get your butt out of here, you cornhusker, and hit behind the pitcher, where you belong!" I was so scared I didn't even take infield that day. About all you could do back then was to cry, which I did when I was alone that night.[4]

He went 0-for-3 against the Washington Senators' Monte Weaver, but notched his first hit the next day off Floyd "General" Crowder. One week later, on September 18, he collected his first major league home run, this off the Boston Red Sox' Gordon Rhodes. The day before that memorable homer, September 17, had provided the young player with a memory that in later years proved more vivid in the form of a brush with baseball royalty.

Gomez gave up only three hits that afternoon, struck out at least one batter in every inning except the fifth, and walked just two in the effort. For Trosky, despite the brush with the immortal Babe Ruth, the day certainly wasn't an unqualified warm and happy memory. "I swung at the first eleven pitches that (Lefty) Gomez threw, and never touched a one. When I ticked the twelfth, the crowd cheered." Trosky lamented when recalling his first four-strikeout game, "Maybe you don't think I was low. That night our manager, Walter Johnson, put his arm around me and said, 'You're going to be my first baseman for a long time.'"[5] In 44 at-bats that month, spread over 11 games, Trosky hit .295 with a homer, a double, and two triples, and drove in eight runs.

His debut completed, Trosky quickly returned to Iowa for the winter. This year, though, he was not heading home just for farmwork and conditioning. He had other, more personal plans in work as well.

On November 15, six weeks following the end of the season and only four days after his 21st birthday, Hal married Lorraine Evelyn Glenn in a ceremony at St. Michael's in Norway. Glenn, the daughter of a veterinarian, was a year ahead of him in school and had never paid much attention to him during their teenage years. She was serious and attractive and had plans for life after high school that didn't involve farming. Trosky, on the other hand, had been a talented athlete, but he was a farm boy at his core. His future, most in town had presumed, at least before the baseball scouts came sniffing around, would involve getting some ground of his own to work and following his father into the farming business. It was the normal life template of that place and time, and Trosky would have happily adopted the path as well. Once he signed a professional baseball contract, though, he was finally able to catch Lorraine's eye.

Hal Trosky getting loose with the bat in a mid–1930s photograph from the *Cleveland Press*. This photograph was taken on the road, away from Cleveland, as the Indians only wore solid-color jerseys at home. After 1940, the team discarded the stripes altogether (Special Collections at Cleveland State University).

Lorraine Glenn was half a semester ahead of Trosky in school, and by late 1933 was already well into her college years in Cedar Rapids, at what is now Mount Mercy University, while studying to become a nurse. He had been visiting her over the winters when the minor league seasons ended, and had finally convinced her to marry him over the previous summer. Lorraine was no shrinking violet—she'd accompany him hunting for pheasant and rabbit, and was no stranger to hard work on the farm, not that she particularly craved the life— and ultimately proved to be the perfect wife for the aspiring baseball star.

❖3❖

Rookie

"How about Trosky?" Walter Johnson enthused to a pack of writers on the eve of the Indians' departure for spring training in New Orleans. "There's a boy who's going to be a great hitter. Whether he's ready for the big leagues I don't know, but until he shows me he isn't I think I'll consider Trosky my first baseman."[1]

In March, the national "Bible of Baseball," J. G. Taylor Spink's weekly *The Sporting News,* opined that "Johnson will reach into a figurative hat containing seven Cleveland Indians, draw out four of them and hope he has an infield … because [Trosky] has the ability to hit, he has been given the call over Harley Boss, a capable fielder who has shown weakness with the willow."[2] Not that the young first baseman was flawless. Far from it, in fact. Young Cleveland outfielder Joe Vosmik watched Trosky over several games, and "finally asked whether he followed the flight of the ball from the pitcher's hand with one or both eyes. Hal confessed blankly that he didn't know."[3] Trosky had an enormous amount of natural, physical talent, but at the big league level, he soon learned that the mind mattered as well.

Gordon Cobbledick noted in the March 11 *Cleveland Plain Dealer* that "[incumbent first baseman Harley] Boss and Trosky appear to be evenly matched, with the former's experience balancing the latter's superior batting power." Trosky began spring training in New Orleans by notching only two hits in his first six exhibition games. Eventually, though, Boss' fragility cost him the job. When Boss succumbed to injury, Trosky opened the Indians' 1934 season as the $3,000-a-year regular first baseman. Boss was sent to the New Orleans Pelicans, in the Class A Southern Association, while Trosky would play every inning of every game that year. Boss would kick about the minors until 1946, but he never returned to the big league stage.

Cleveland fans had high hopes as the Indians broke camp and rode the train north. Johnson was planning to start the youngest infield in Cleveland history. Trosky, at first base, had just turned 21; Boze Berger and Bill Knickerbocker were both 22; and the senior statesman was third baseman Odell "Bad News" Hale, relatively wizened at 25. Throughout the early part of the season, Cleveland coaches and infielders met early each day to work on defensive fundamentals and to develop cohesiveness. Trosky found this time especially valuable, a continuation of Steve O'Neill's tutelage the previous year at Toledo, and he eventually began to play into acceptable form. Willis Hudlin, for one, noted that as a pitcher he benefitted greatly from Trosky's big bat, but periodically also suffered from fielding miscues.

Back in January, the team had purchased some fresh faces to compete for jobs, absorbing the contracts of Trosky, Ralph Winegarner, Thornton Lee, Milt Galatzar, and Monte Pearson, among others, from Toledo.[4] By the end of spring, though, Johnson had finally settled on a lineup that included Frankie Pytlak behind the plate, an infield of Trosky, Hale, Knickerbocker, and veteran Willie Kamm, and an outfield of Averill, Vosmik and 44-year-old, future Hall of Famer Sam Rice, who had been released by the Senators in January. On paper, when coupled with a pitching rotation of Mel Harder, Pearson, Oral Hildebrand, and Hudlin, the team didn't look half bad. It was not necessarily ready to knock off the Tigers or the Yankees, but it looked like a competitive product, one that would actually entice fans to buy tickets and attend games.

The previous year, despite the presence of the huge waterfront facility that was Cleveland Municipal Stadium, with a capacity for more than 70,000 per game, the Indians had drawn fewer than 400,000 fans through the turnstiles for the entire season. That direct revenue shortfall ultimately led Alva Bradley to try to cut the pay of GM Evans from $30,000 to a reported $12,500, and Evans quit rather than accept the reduction. Bradley was desperate to field a squad that could lure ticket buyers back to the park.

The 1934 Indians were scheduled to open the regular season on April 17 in Cleveland against the historically hapless St. Louis Browns. The imposing Indians triumvirate of Averill (who had also been forced to take a pay cut),[5] Vosmik and Trosky filled the 3–4–5 slots in the batting order, and the local papers figuratively drooled over the potentially explosive lineup. Their frenzy was fanned by the prospect of returning to "friendly" (translation: "tiny") League Park.

League Park

One of the peripheral distractions confronting the Indians in the 1930s was their ballpark situation. They had two from which to choose, and the selection had an impact on the team's style of play. Both the team and the entire region celebrated, as a portent of growth and expansion, the 1931 opening of Cleveland Municipal Stadium. The new park was enormous, yet the historical baseball headquarters of the city stood three miles away, in the shape of League Park, built in 1891 at the corner of Dunham Street (later East 66th) and Lexington Avenue. It took its name from National League Park, at Cedar Avenue and East 49th, which had been the home field for the Cleveland Spiders from 1879–1884.

The owner of the Indians at the time had been a gifted business-man and opportunist, so it was small surprise when Frank DeHaas Robison and his brother Stanley elected to build a baseball park at their trolley stop at East 66th Street and Lexington Avenue. They moved the team from the previous site at the intersection of Euclid and Payne in an attempt to grow both ballpark attendance and trolley ridership.

On May 1, 1891, at just after 4 p.m., Cy Young opened the Cleveland Spiders' National League season against Cincinnati and, in doing so, consecrated the new League Park III. Because of a zoning requirement that it fit within the existing neighborhood street geometry (the field was originally built around a saloon and two other houses whose owners refused to sell their land when the park was conceived), League was oddly shaped. It boasted a 353-foot left-field line but a right-field fence that, a mere 290 feet from home plate, seemingly brushed against the infield grass. There was also very little foul territory, so the fans were almost in the midst of the action.

In 1903 the Indians added bleachers in front of the right-field fence and stands in left field outside the playing area. The right-field bleachers were gone by 1908. Osborn Engineering, the most prominent designer of ballparks at the time, was contracted to make the stadium safer, more spacious, and generally more accommodating to paying customers. On April 21, 1910, the new and improved League Park IV reopened, capable of accommodating 24,414 fans. The business offices were located upstairs, above the ticket office, and were as cramped as the bullpens, which were wedged between the foul lines and bleachers in right and left fields (the Indians used the first-base side).

The western dimension, the right-field line, was built along East 66th Street, while left field ran along Linwood Avenue. In the outfield, East 70th Street bordered the east face from left field to center field. Still only 290 feet down the right-field line (240 feet if roped off for big games), it expanded in a rectangle to a farthest reach of 460 feet just left of straightaway center field (this was shortened to 420 feet in a 1920 renovation). The left-field line extended 375 feet at the pole. Even with the unusual dimensions, though, League was certainly a Jewel Box ballpark.

The concrete and steel ballparks that were built beginning in the early 20th century, largely to replace the older, wooden ones (largely fire hazards like League I, and with less seating capacity) are now collectively referred to as the Jewel Box ballparks. Philadelphia was home to the progenitor of the class, Baker Bowl (1895), as well as one of the early, true Jewel Boxes in Shibe Park (1909). Some of the greatest moments in baseball history played out in Jewel Box parks like Ebbets Field, Forbes Field (Pittsburgh), and Griffith Stadium (Washington, D.C.), but with the exceptions of Fenway Park in Boston and Wrigley Field in Chicago, those quirky, urban parks have been consigned to history. With the exceptions of Shibe and Comiskey (Chicago) Parks, those Jewel Boxes were all built amid the physical limitations of existing city blocks, which resulted in similarly quirky, often asymmetrical outfields.

In 1920 the park underwent a partial renovation as dimensions were changed slightly by the addition of outfield bleachers, and a wall was erected along the right-field boundary. Prevailing winds tended to carry batted balls to left, but even with strong gusts it was difficult to knock the ball out of the yard.

The right-field fence, if not truly monstrous, was certainly odd. The first 20 feet above the ground were solid wall, and on top of that was a 25-foot-tall wire mesh fence with steel stanchions along the border. In all, the fence was 45 feet high, in contrast with Fenway Park's left field "Green Monster," which rises 37 feet. In 1934, perhaps because of the unique abilities of young left-handed slugger Hal Trosky, the screen was lowered five feet, leaving the barrier an even 40 feet high. The fun began when balls failed to clear the wall. A ball hitting the fence at League might have hit the solid wall and bounced predictably; it might have struck the chicken-wire mesh and died; or it might have hit a stanchion and caromed in any direction. There are numerous anecdotes of balls that hit the fence less than a foot apart, one falling limply to the ground after hitting the mesh, and the next bouncing almost all the way back to second base in a ricochet off one of the metal posts.

The field had no permanent lights, so night games were not an option, but there was one such contest there, on July 27, 1931. Using a portable lighting system borrowed from the Kansas City Monarchs and designed by Iowan J. L. Wilkinson, the Homestead Grays of the Negro National League played the barnstorming House of David team in the first (and only) night contest at League.

In 1928, after using old League Park for nearly two decades, the voters of Cleveland approved a bond issue for the financing of a stadium to he built on a landfill off of Lake Erie. The edifice, when finished, seated over 78,000 customers, and was a vast fly-ball graveyard for hitters. It covered 12 acres and had been designed by the same engineering firm responsible for Yankee Stadium and Fenway Park. The foul poles were over 320 feet from home plate, but quickly expanded to a cavernous 435 feet in the power alleys and 420 feet in center field. These distances, coupled with generous foul territory and the "gentle breezes" off the lake, made a hitter's job brutally difficult.

At the time Municipal Stadium closed, following the 1993 season, no player had ever hit a home run to straightaway center field. It was not that players of that era weren't capable of power hitting; Babe Ruth once hit a hall at League Park that was reportedly a line drive that was still rising when it impacted the center field scoreboard 420 feet away. While tales of home run distances were often exaggerated at the time, especially when ascribing some mythological quality to blasts by sluggers like Ruth or Josh Gibson, there is no arguing that some of those men were capable of hitting a baseball a very long way. That the dimensions of Municipal Stadium, and the effects of Lake Erie's exhalations, kept anyone from knocking one over the center field fence is as much an indictment of the ballpark as it is a judgment of the players.

The Indians played all of their games in 1934 and 1935, and most of 1936, at League, but slowly began to use the municipal park more and more as the crowds increased and the social center of town moved toward the Terminal area. By 1947, Bill Veeck was scheduling all of the games downtown, and League Park finally closed in 1948. Back in 1934, though, it was a very friendly home for a big, left-handed power hitter.

The 1934 Season

The Troskys, within a few weeks of the start of the season, had moved into a comfortable home in East Cleveland. Lorraine did most of the work involved with the transition, which left Hal free to concentrate on his duties at first base. He and teammate Billy Sullivan (a man smart enough, motivated enough, and affluent enough to attend law school in the off-season, while most players worked just to pay the bills) carpooled to the park, and Trosky began to make friends with some of the veterans. Pitcher Mel Harder took the young slugger under his wing, allowing the 21-year-old's quiet and congenial personality to integrate him gently into the Indians' clubhouse.

The Cleveland sportswriters were not yet sold on Trosky's potential, and several wondered publicly whether Slapnicka's young project would ever pan out. In the locker room, Trosky still burned with the memory of his public failure the preceding September at the hands of Lefty Gomez, and he obviously wanted nothing more than to contribute to his new team and earn some respect. On April 24, he finally showed a hint of his potential.

Having taken a tip from relief pitcher George Connally one afternoon, that he switch to a lighter bat in order to better get around on major league pitching,[6] Trosky punished Irving "Bump" Hadley and the Browns' bullpen for four hits, including two home runs, and six RBI. Both home runs came with two men on base, the first clearing the right-field pavilion roof in St Louis and nearly crossing the adjacent road, and the second hitting the far edge of the roof and bouncing out of the park. Trosky's display was part of a 19-hit Cleveland explosion and helped Oral Hildebrand coast to a 15–2 win.

Collectively, the city of Cleveland sat up and took notice of the "Bohemian Blaster" (so dubbed by Cobbledick) from Iowa. After 32 games, thanks to a string of 13 hits in 28 at-bats, he was hitting .304 with five home runs and 26 RBIs. On May 23 the Indians lost a wild two-run decision to the Red Sox after Boston staged a three-run, ninth-inning rally. It killed the momentum generated from a (rare) Indians three-game sweep of the Yankees, and wasted Trosky's home run and double off yet another future Hall of Famer, Lefty Grove. On May 30, Trosky silenced the doubters by slamming three consecutive home runs in the second game of a League Park doubleheader against the White Sox.

Those three homers gave Trosky the early season league lead in that department, passing teammate Averill's seven with that final blow. One of the remarkable aspects of Trosky's big afternoon was his relative youth. The only other 21-year-old, at the time, to accomplish the feat had been Mel Ott in 1931. Since that afternoon, only Al Kaline and Eddie Mathews—both 20—and former Orioles slugger Boog Powell have recorded three-homer games at age 21 or younger. Joe DiMaggio, Mickey Cochrane and modern phenom Bryce Harper didn't reach the plateau until they were 22.

In a *Plain-Dealer* sidebar, Cobbledick opined that "At 21, the young first baseman has a dozen years ahead of him in which he should spread terror among opposing pitchers—increasing terror as the seasons pass. He won't be King Babe II, but he may be Prince Hal I."[7] After the game, Billy Evans telegraphed Cy Slapnicka in Cedar Rapids, sharing the news about Trosky's big afternoon at the plate. On May 31, Slapnicka took a break from scouting long enough to send a brief telegram back to the Cleveland writers who, just weeks earlier, had dared doubt the sage's judgment. The message was succinct: "HEAVY CANNONADING HEARD FROM LEAGUE PARK. WHAT ABOUT TROSKY NOW?"

Despite Slapnicka's justifiable smugness in response to a press corps that had doubted the scout's judgment regarding his slugging prospect, Trosky was certainly not the first to smack three home runs in a single game. Ned Williamson recorded the first three-homer game—in what can be considered the "major leagues"–on Memorial Day in 1884. Playing for the Chicago White Stockings (later the Cubs, not the White Sox) in tiny Lake Park in Chicago, with a right field fence no more than 230 feet from home plate (more likely less than 200 feet), Williamson lofted three fly balls over the wall.[8] He actually parlayed that unique situation into enduring fame: In a 13-year career in which Williamson logged only 64 career homers, 27 of those came in that

1884 season at Lake Park. The "27" figure was recognized as baseball's single-season home run record for 36 years, until Babe Ruth hit 29 in 1919. Williamson's record was clearly a ballpark-induced aberration, as he never hit more than nine home runs in a season. Ruth, on the other hand, broke his own record the following year, with 54 homers in 1920.

Regarding Williamson, the immortal Cap Anson duplicated Williamson's three-homer game mark less than three months later, again at Lake Park, a feat that prompted the *Boston Herald* to note of the latter's effort, "on any other league grounds, Anson's three home runs of August 6 would be about three singles. That over-the-fence rule is a perfect sham and burlesque, and should not deceive baseball readers."[9] By the time Trosky enjoyed his first three-homer game, 50 years later, 40 different major league batters had also reached that mark, with nine of those before 1901 when ballparks weren't as "dimensionally consistent" from one to another. There was an explosion of three-homer games in the 1920s, with Ty Cobb joining the club in 1925, Lou Gehrig doing it twice, and Ruth going one better by doing it twice in World Series games. The only other Indian to have achieved that feat, in an organization whose roster had at times included Nap LaJoie, Joe Jackson, and Tris Speaker, was Trosky's teammate, the still relatively underappreciated center fielder, Earl Averill.

"The Earl of Snohomish"

Howard Earl Averill grew up in baseball Siberia, in Snohomish, Washington, about an hour's drive north of Seattle. Born in 1902, he attended public schools and played baseball on a local semi-pro team, the Snohomish Pilchuckers, before finally earning a shot with the San Francisco Seals in the Pacific Coast League in 1926.

In those days, the PCL was an interesting baseball biome. It offered quasi-major league competition by giving aging big league stars a few more years; one of Averill's teammates was 40-year-old Ping Bodie, whose major league career had spanned nine seasons with the White Sox and Yankees, among others. But the league also provided a launching pad for up-and-coming talent; one of Averill's teammates was a 17-year-old Frank Crosetti, the future two-time All-Star who would hold down the Yankees' shortstop job for 14 years during their dynastic period. Joe DiMaggio even started in the Coast League, and with the same team, a few years later in 1932. Averill was clearly one of the latter group, a talented and younger player, so the Seals were reluctant to let him go.

By the time the Indians finally purchased Averill's contract in 1929, they gave him the starting center field job outright. In his first big league at-bat, Averill homered off none other than Earl Whitehill, and for the season batted .332 in 152 games.

At only 5'9½", Averill did not look the part of slugger, but with his powerful shoulders and arms he became a feared line-drive hitter. Nicknamed "Rock" by his peers, he remains one of the best, and least appreciated, hitters in Cleveland Indians history. As of 2015, he is still ranked eighth in career batting average (.322), fifth in slugging percentage, and is the franchise leader in runs, total bases, runs batted in, and triples. In an organization that boasts of an alumni club with names like Tris Speaker and Nap Lajoie, Averill's achievements (all compiled between 1929 and 1939) are even more impressive.

Any discussion of Cleveland baseball that does not include the six-time American League All-Star is incomplete. Period. Unfortunately, the event most often attached to Averill's name is the notorious line drive that he hit off Dizzy Dean, breaking the pitcher's toe, in the 1937 All-Star Game. Dean tried to come back from the injury too soon and compensated for the pain by altering his pitching mechanics. Those changes shorted Dean's career drastically, effectively forcing him out of action entirely at age 31.

Averill himself lasted in the majors until 1941. The Indians traded him to Detroit in 1939, but at age 37 and not fully recovered from an earlier back injury, the slugger was more of a shadow than the feared hitter he had been. Earl and his wife Lotte retired to Washington after baseball, and he operated a motel there for several decades. He was elected to the Baseball Hall of Fame in 1975, and passed away from pneumonia in 1981.

Mid-Summer

Despite splitting the May 30 doubleheader, Cleveland retained a one-and-a-half-game lead over New York and a two-game advantage over Detroit in the American League standings. It was a nice position for the Indians as they entered June. On June 14, Trosky continued his barrage by driving in six runs with two homers against the A's at Shibe Park in Philadelphia, saving his best for last. The score was tied 7–7 in the ninth inning when Trosky stepped up to the plate. With two outs, Philly pitcher Bob Kline found himself in a corner, behind in the count with three balls and one strike. In such a bases-loaded situation, late in a tied game, not only did Trosky know what was coming next, but so did everyone in attendance. At that moment, a pitcher has to throw a strike, and there is only one pitch that can consistently be put in the strike zone: a fastball.

Kline did not disappoint. Neither did Trosky. The slugger turned and smashed it high and deep over the 12-foot-high right field wall and out on to 20th Street. Shibe Park had the deepest center field in baseball at 468 feet (seven feet deeper than the acreage in Yankee Stadium), but the right field fence was a mere 331 feet from the plate—not nearly far enough to contain such a blast.

Trosky's slugging numbers continued to grow, but his fielder's mitt too often betrayed him. In a late-July game in which he drove in five runs and scored two more against the same Athletics, he fumbled a slow-rolling ground hall in the ninth inning, setting up the winning rally. Although the Indians would not have even been in the game without Trosky's bat, it was the first baseman's glove that determined the outcome.

With 51 games left to play, the Indians were 9½ games behind first-place Detroit. This year, however, there would be no catching the Tigers juggernaut. The Cleveland offense was cruising, and five starters finished the season with batting averages over .300, but the young infield made more than its share of errors, and the Indians—despite 85 victories—closed the season 16 games out of first place.

After the season, New York sportswriter Dan Daniel dubbed Hal Trosky his unofficial American League Rookie of the Year for 1934. Trosky, Daniel wrote, "was eager, ambitious, and he never forgot. He was determined to stick. And stick he did ... as the campaign progressed, Hal became a steadier, more graceful fielder and a powerful, dangerous hitter. He is a left-handed hitter, who can pull the ball to hellandgone [sic]."[10]

Hal Trosky had played every inning of all 154 games and finished seventh in balloting for American League Most Valuable Player. It was a tough ballot: Even Triple Crown winner Lou Gehrig finished in fifth place as the award went to Mickey Cochrane, catcher-manager of the pennant-winning Detroit Tigers.

A few days after Cleveland's final out of the year, Hal and Lorraine packed up their still-meager belongings and headed west to Iowa for a winter of farming, family, and relative anonymity. His hometown was proud that, while the boy did have a vice (chewing tobacco), the strongest language he had ever used in public was "dickens." He was a wonderful ambassador from Norway to the world, and his neighbors recognized him generously.

Dan Daniel stirred the figurative pot over that winter. Stoking the fires of the informal hot stove league, he wrote a column which quoted Yankees president Ed Barrow as saying: "Hal Trosky has the best chance to succeed Lou Gehrig as the power house of the American League, and was far-and-away the outstanding recruit of 1934.... Trosky is a greater ball player than Hank Greenberg and will develop faster in all departments."[11] This was heady praise from the respected Barrow and fostered a career-long infatuation between Trosky and New York. Several times over the next decade, the Yankees would approach Trosky about the prospect of donning the pinstripes, but the timing was never quite right. Lorraine Trosky recalled encouraging Hal to sign with New York in 1943 after a year-long sabbatical, but he did not feel up to dealing with a tour of duty inside the Big Apple's media fishbowl.

The comments by Barrow, incidentally, were clipped by Tigers owner Frank Navin and sent to Greenberg during salary negotiations over the off-season. Although Greenberg and Trosky evidently deeply respected each other's ability, the two would be extremely competitive rivals and only coolly distant acquaintances over the following years.

The subsequent off-season was different from any that Hal Trosky had ever enjoyed. As a young star in the national pastime, his presence became a valuable commodity for others. One Saturday in January 1935, Newman's Department Store in Cedar Rapids hired Trosky to sign autographs. They ran a six-inch ad in the Cedar Rapids papers, advertising that "The hard-hitting hero of the Cleveland Indians ... will autograph your baseball. Bring an old one or buy one at Newman's. Hear what the 'big gun' of baseballdom has to say about the game. He will answer your questions! This is a real treat!" The copy may not have been up to the slick standards of modern advertising, but the attraction of the "hook" was unmistakable. Hal Trosky had arrived.

On October 18, Trosky's hometown held a special Thursday evening celebration for their new favorite son. The Norway Commercial Club put together an evening to celebrate Trosky's rookie year with, in addition to a program of accordion selections—a staple of Bohemian émigré' culture in America—and a cowboy singer, an array of local speakers who lectured the community on topics such as "character building (through baseball)" and "baseball in Korea." The final two spots in the lineup included a special talk on "old time baseball" by none other than Billy Hoffer, and finally Trosky's own remarks. Hoffer's presence was all the more special because until that time he was the finest professional ballplayer to emerge from the greater Cedar Rapids area. There are no notes or newspaper accounts of Hoffer's speech, but his attendance and sanction effectively conferred his place of honor to young Trosky.

Trosky spoke only briefly that night, feeling very much the shy 21-year-old facing his elders. He praised the Indians and thanked fellow sluggers Ruth and Foxx for their invaluable advice and kindness. The good feeling would keep bringing him back to Iowa after every baseball season he would ever play.

Hal Trosky stretching out for a throw at first base in Cleveland. Although often maligned for his defense early in his career, Trosky's diligent practice made him a more-than-adequate glove man later in his career (*Cleveland Press* Collection, Michael Schwartz Library, Cleveland State University).

Sophomore Slump

[He was] a very nice man, a gentleman. I had to be careful to keep the ball inside, and keep him from getting those long arms extended. Didn't want him getting a full swing on the ball. He could hit it a long, long way.

—Elden Auker[1]

Although the Indians had settled for a third-place finish, from a selfish, Trosky-centric perspective the 1934 season had been nothing less than a monstrous success. Hal and Lorraine returned to Norway and settled in for a winter of farm chores while getting reacquainted with their hometown, this time as a celebrity couple. Unfortunately, the Depression had forced a degree of compromise on almost every family in the country, and young, budding star baseball players were no different. As a concession to the times, the Troskys shared their off-season in a home with the future Norway school superintendent, Carsten Johnston, and his wife. Those sorts of accommodations were not unusual, and the two couples remained close friends for years after.

Trosky added a regimen of ice skating and wood chopping to maintain his condition throughout the winter. Although the nation remained in the grip of a multi-year heating pattern in the climate, the same phenomenon that fomented the "dust bowl" in the western states, outdoor exercise in Iowa was not always easy. The Midwestern United States is notorious for general misery between January and March, so perhaps "warm" is not the most descriptive adjective for the winter of 1933–1934, but Trosky was undaunted by the snow and ice. The February 10 edition of the *Cleveland Plain Dealer* ran a human-interest feature on the Troskys that ran nearly two-thirds of a page, showing images of Hal chopping wood (wearing a fedora and collared shirt, no less), a full-length portrait of a seated Lorraine, and an article replete with the expected pre-season enthusiasm for the upcoming year.

The piece, entitled: "Indians Are Best, Yanks Rate Second, Says Trosky," quoted Trosky directly. "Cleveland's husky first baseman declared the ... Yankees and the champion Detroit Tigers would be tough, but repeated his assertion that the Indians were the class of the field."[2] Interestingly, the article later noted that, at age 22, "Trosky is still an unspoiled kid, who can't quite believe that he's a real big-leaguer. He speaks almost reverently of the older heads in the game.... He also expressed admiration for Walter Johnson as a manager and a man." The article not only offered a bit of insight into Trosky's character and how he spent his off-season, but was crafted in such a way as to stoke the hot stove for the fans in Cleveland.

Trosky offered an anecdote that revealed both his humor and humility, describing a particularly memorable interaction with the only umpire who had troubled him. "Bill McGowan was working behind the plate one day. I noticed he'd been kind of grouchy all afternoon, and I heard afterwards he had a stomach ache, but I didn't know that soon enough. All I did was look at him and he growled. 'Don't look at me like that. No rookie can look at me.' Believe me, I didn't look again."[3]

The 1935 edition of the Indians arrived in New Orleans for spring training with heady visions of a pennant. Why New Orleans? Once again, the world outside baseball intruded into the business of the game. The concept of sending teams off-site for spring training began in the late nineteenth century, when players would show up truly out of shape after a winter of working at other jobs, and with each team arranging a unique location, there was nothing of the structure and game schedule that exists today. The Indians trained in New Orleans from 1928–1939 for a number of reasons, but mainly because infamous Louisiana politico Huey Long wanted them there.

In late 1935, and a month after "the Kingfish," as Long was—and is—known, was assassinated inside the state capitol building in Baton Rouge, Ed Bang wrote that the "Tribe has trained in New Orleans for so long it seemed like a permanent arrangement. Much of the preference for the Crescent City, however, was inspired by the late Huey Long's interest in the Indians." Before his firing in late 1935, general manager Billy Evans had "practically completed arrangements to train on the west coast, but Long prevailed on the owners to return to New Orleans."[4]

Hal Trosky made it to Louisiana and baseball fully renewed after an invigorating winter in Iowa, bolstered by both a $1,000 raise (roughly $13,000 in 2015 dollars) and genuine self-confidence in his ability to hit big league pitching. As a bonus, his mentor from Toledo—Steve O'Neill—had been hired as a Cleveland coach.

The Sporting News acknowledged that the Indians had a shot at the pennant, highlighting the fact that five of the eight projected regulars in Cleveland's lineup batted over .300 in 1934.[5] While Lorraine again took charge of moving the Trosky household items back to Shaker Heights, Hal picked up where he'd left off at the plate. Even Connie Mack jumped on the bandwagon. "In Trosky," he stated in a speech to Philadelphia fans and writers, "the Indians have a wonderful young first baseman. He promises to be Ruth's successor in baseball, and as he goes, so will go the Cleveland club. It depends solely upon him, to my way of thinking, whether Cleveland finishes first or last."[6]

A smiling Trosky, fresh off the heels of his dazzling 1934 rookie season. After batting .330 with 35 homers and driving in 142 runs, the game had to have seemed easy for the young Iowan. Little did he know, when this photograph was taken, how different the upcoming 1935 season would feel (*Cleveland Press* Collection, Michael Schwartz Library, Cleveland State University).

Then reality intruded.

With a vengeance.

All of those superlative-laden pre-season expectations came crashing down about the ears of the Cleveland fans as the regular season progressed and the games started to matter. The Indians began the campaign strongly, with five of their first six victories coming in one-run games, but Trosky took seven games to find his home run stroke. As in 1934, Trosky waited until the Indians were engaged in a battle with the Browns to flash his power.

This time, Cleveland trailed St Louis, 6–5, in the seventh inning when Earl Averill led off with a single. Trosky then smashed Ivy Paul Andrews' offering over the center field fence. His heroics garnered him a headline in Cleveland in bold one-inch letters. It seemed to energize the sophomore's bat for a brief time, but Trosky was actually focusing most of his concentration on his fielding. Around the league, pundits and players alike judged that he had improved his glove-work significantly over the previous year.

Trosky quickly upped his home run total to four, the last coming against the White Sox as the Tribe ended the South-Siders' six-game winning streak, but despite the spasms of optimism the Indians never really got on track. An 8–1 start sagged to a 20–15 record by the end of May, and once again the writers were becoming restless.

Manager Walter Johnson, honeymoon phase over, was becoming an issue in the local press, taking his share (and perhaps a bit more) of the blame for the team's moribund start and perceived lack of effort. There was, unsurprisingly, no top cover for Johnson from the front office. *Washington Post* sports editor Shirley Povich later attributed many of Cleveland's difficulties to their owner, Alva Bradley. In 1940, Povich termed Bradley a "vacillating, mouse-like owner" who was a great business man but a very poor baseball man. When Bradley fired Roger Peckinpaugh, he stated that "we only hire the manager; the public fires him."[7]

According to Fred Lewis, the entire pitching staff was grumbling about Johnson's decision making,[8] but that was likely speculative exaggeration. Willis Hudlin later remembered feeling like the young infield may have hurt him (as a sinker ball pitcher), as balls that more experienced fielders might have reeled in somehow squirted through to the outfield. On May 23, all hell broke loose. Johnson openly confronted Willie Kamm and catcher Glenn Myatt about fomenting an anti–Johnson faction on the team, and ordered Kamm to return to Cleveland in the midst of a road trip. He also had Myatt released. Cleveland fans, given the choice of supporting manager or players, blamed Johnson.[9]

That particular episode gained so much public traction that even

4. *Sophomore Slump*

Commissioner Landis was pulled into the abyss. The *Cleveland News* reported that Kamm reported the attack on his reputation to the commissioner's office and actually met with Landis himself as he tried to repair his reputation. "The commissioner ruled, in effect," continued the story, "that [Johnson and Kamm] are both nice boys of excellent character and reputation, but they just can't get along together. It's too bad, but I can't do anything about it."[10]

In a futile attempt to close this iteration of Pandora's Box and suppress the talk of dissension, 21 of the players ran an advertisement in local papers entitled "Some Inside Stuff Direct From the Camp of the Indians." The ad carried a page of alibi-ing for the internal turmoil and swore to the public that the team was not rife with dissension. The players' facsimile signatures appeared at the bottom of the page.

Just as it is impossible to un-ring a bell, this particular ploy did not elicit the intended effect.

Two days later, in early June, the team returned to League Park and the crowd booed the manager yet again. Trosky, as the team's slugging leader, did not escape the public blame either. He was suffering the first significant, extended slump of his baseball career. "Hal's worry over his slump is moderated only slightly by the fact he knows what is wrong. There's a hitch in his swing. Instead of bringing his bat down from his shoulder and swinging it smoothly into the path of the ball, Hal stops the swing, takes his hitch, then follows through—usually a bit too late."[11]

Trosky got slump-busting advice from everyone, but to little avail. "Gehrig told me not to let it worry me. That he and everybody else has been through the same thing. But it's awful hard to be up there, knowing the team needs that hit, and be unable to make it. I know that I can hit. If I thought I was only a .250 hitter I wouldn't feel so bad about it. I've always hit and I have the confidence that I can." The first baseman even experimented with a right-handed stance in batting practice, putting at least one ball into the stands, but was hesitant to try it in a real game. Ed Bang later observed that "Hal was a worried man. He's that type, and the Indians were so desperately short-handed on account of illness and injuries that they couldn't give [him] the long rest he obviously needed."[12]

Still, the Indians were unable to right their ship. By the end of July, Alva Bradley could bury his head in the sand no deeper, unable to ignore the issue. He summoned Johnson and told the pitching great that he was being replaced at the helm by O'Neill. Johnson, a man worthy of his enormous reputation, told the owner to wait until the end of the next road trip. "We're going on a short Western trip and we'll probably lose a lot of games. It wouldn't be fair to O'Neill to have him start on a losing streak. I'll take the club west and you can announce my resignation the minute we get hack, regardless of the success or failure of the trip."[13]

In his monumental opus, *The Cleveland Indians Encyclopedia*, Russell Schneider succinctly captured the mood of the day. Schneider observed that Ed Bang, sports editor of the *Cleveland News*, had written the previous year that "Johnson showed anything but mental alertness and managerial ability ... he fell so far short of what a wide-awake manager should do that the fans who were wont to cheer him ... groaned in despair and booed him."[14] The savagery of the collective Cleveland press is largely inexplicable, given Johnson's demeanor and stature in the game (he would be elected to the Hall of Fame the following year). The "Big Train" had managed the Senators for four years before coming to Cleveland, winning more than 90 games in three of those years. In his final year in Washington, Johnson skippered the team to a 93–61 record (and a third-place finish) before being shown the door by Calvin Griffith simply because the owner believed Johnson "lacked something in his character to manage a pennant winner."[15]

Walter Johnson managed his final major league game on Sunday, August 4, at Navin Field in Detroit. Perhaps fittingly, Trosky knocked one of only four Cleveland hits on the day, a fourth-inning single, but also logged an error in a 7–0 loss to the Tigers. Trosky's day at the plate was an apt microcosm of Johnson's time in Cleveland. In parts of two seasons and a full 1934 effort, he skippered the Tribe to a 179–168 record, a .516 winning percentage. Professional sports have always carried a "what have you done for me lately" sort of ethos, and even in 1935 a winning record alone was insufficient job security. The obsequious Bradley appears to have been more concerned about public perception than about actual results.

From the beginning, Alva Bradley was a man somewhat ill-suited to the stewardship of the Indians. As Franklin Lewis wrote, upon learning that a group of his wealthy peers and friends were looking to buy the team in 1927 and told him that they'd selected him to be club president,

Bradley reportedly responded, "I'm certainly the man most qualified to be president, as I know nothing whatever about baseball."[16] Born into privilege in Cleveland in 1884, Bradley left Ohio for the Ivy League and graduated from Cornell with the class of 1908. He returned to manage the family real estate business and served as president and treasurer of the United States Coal Company.[17] While an avid sports enthusiast by reputation, and by many accounts an executive who could communicate with players on a one-on-one basis, he was not an astute leader of a major league baseball organization.

Perhaps hobbled by exaggerated pre-season expectations and an acerbic local press, or possibly simply out of boredom, Bradley had hired Johnson to replace Roger Peckinpaugh just two years earlier despite "Peck's" 26–25 record. Now it was Johnson's turn to pay the price. Johnson' successor, Steve O'Neill, would go on to post winning seasons in 1936 and 1937 before getting the proverbial ax, and O'Neill's replacement, Ossie Vitt, would preside over one of the epic team melt-downs in major league history before also being fired.

No, Alva Bradley was a smart man, just not a smart owner.

In hiring Steve O'Neill, at least Bradley had returned to the people of Cleveland a legitimate home-team hero. O'Neill had been a catcher during his playing days, and his best season had come as the Indians' catcher during the magical 1920 season, the only World Series victory for the team. O'Neill batted .333 with two doubles in that seven-game tilt and handled a pitching staff that included Tribe legends Stan Coveleski, Jim Bagby, and even a young George Uhle. "There probably is no one who would deny the Indians might have won the [1935] pennant if they had had the O'Neill of 1920."[18] That he had coached several of the players on the current roster during his Toledo tenure was an unstated but unmistakable asset as well.

And, for a time, the team responded. The Indians won five of their first eight games under O'Neill and finished August with a 19–14 record. Trosky, however, was never quite able to recapture the consistent batting form that had served him so well as a rookie. It was a hard lesson in big league baseball, and it demanded that the young star grow up or get out of the game.

In the heart of the maelstrom, however, Hal Trosky was maturing. Writer Ed McAuley profiled the slugger in the June 18, 1935, *Cleveland News*:

Hal told me much of his personal life, of his plans and ambitions, of complete happiness of his marriage. He asked me, with naivete which almost made me blush, which Cleveland newspaper would be best for him to send back to Iowa. He was—and is—a big kid with a clean heart, fully worthy of every success that comes his way. The polite shyness of those early days is gone, of course. Trosky speaks his piece now, loud and confidently. He is the team's slowest poker player—and one of its most successful. But when such quicker shufflers as Thornton Lee try to make him hurry his betting or his draw, he tells them in language strong and simple what they can do about it.

I suppose there is no one on the team of whom this writer has been more critical than of Trosky. Yet where at least one of the Indians is definitely hostile and others are cool as a result of these dispatches, Trosky remains friendly and undisturbed. A big man knows how to take it, for he realizes that today's caustic barb is tomorrow's tribute, if he has the stuff—and if he hasn't, he doesn't belong up here anyway.... Trosky can use the long-delayed plaudits of the crowd. They won't go to his head.

"You're not standing the way you used to when you were banging out those long drives for me in Toledo," new manager Steve O'Neill told Trosky one day during batting practice in mid–August. The pair tinkered with his open stance a bit, changing his setup by bringing the right foot closer to home and more in line with the body, then took some of the violent rotation out of his follow-through.[19] Defenses had begun to implement a shift when Trosky came to bat, and mechanical adjustments gave him a better opposite-field approach. After that little chat, the slugger went on a rampage. He belted five home runs in the next ten games, including a grand slam off Washington's Bump Hadley, but with 34 games to go he was still 13 homers off his rookie season pace. The Indians were 17½ games behind Detroit, but only closed the deficit to 11 over the final month.

On August 31, in heat and humidity unique to the Midwest in late summer, White Sox rookie pitcher Vern Kennedy even tossed indignity, in the shape of a no-hitter, at Cleveland. The Indians nearly broke the spell in the ninth inning, but Al Simmons snared Milt Galatzar's one-out, sinking line drive, and after an Averill walk, Joe Vosmik's swinging strikeout on a full count snuffed out any hope of an attempted rally.

The season might have closed quietly after that, but September yielded a couple of odd, remarkable events. The first came on September 7 at Fenway Park in an otherwise meaningless late-season contest between two teams gagging on Detroit's figurative exhaust fumes. With Cleveland ahead 5–3 in the bottom of the ninth, and Oral Hildebrand pitching in relief of Mel Harder, Boston's shortstop/manager Joe Cronin stepped up to bat.

Alan "Dusty" Cooke, Bill Werber, and Mel Almada had loaded the bases, with no outs, for Cronin with three successive singles. Cronin offered at Hildebrand's third pitch and smashed a line drive directly to third baseman Odell Hale. "Bad News" proved to be an apt moniker for the infielder, though, as the smash tore through his glove, smacked off his forehead, and ricocheted toward shortstop Bill Knickerbocker. Once the hall bounced off Hale, staggering the third baseman, all three runners took off for their next destined post. Incredibly, the carom fell into Knickerbocker's glove on the fly to eliminate Cronin. The shortstop fired a dart to Roy Hughes, who had instinctively scrambled to cover second base. "Sage" took the ball cleanly, touched the bag for out number two, and executed a textbook pivot-and-throw to Trosky at first.

The "Triple Play" infield: *from left,* Odell "Bad News" Hale, Bill Knickerbocker, Roy "Sage" Hughes and Hal Trosky, the mainstays of Cleveland's defense in the mid–1930s (Leslie Jones Collection, Boston Public Library).

The throw, a routine infield practice toss, beat the stunned Almada back to the base to complete a surreal triple play.

The second out-of-the-ordinary event took place on September 15. Trosky had fallen into a late-season slump and was spending more and more of his free time brooding. One hit in 41 at-bats will do that to a player. Later, he revealed, he lost almost 20 pounds during the season, due largely to what was diagnosed as an ulcer. He never proffered that as an excuse for his hitting failure, instead swearing that his troubles arose from his "trying too hard" and not relaxing in the batter's box. Regardless, O'Neill collared him the day before and got his attention: "Listen, Hal, they're going to pitch a couple of lefthanders tomorrow. Why don't you turn around and bat right-handed? I've seen you hit that way [at Toledo] and I know you can do it."

Trosky reportedly responded, "I guess I might as well. I can't be any worse than I am now."[20]

Overall, for the doubleheader, Trosky had five hits in ten at-bats (from both sides of the plate), including a double and a home run. The press loved it. "Elated over the success of his noble experiment, Hal Trosky ... today declared that he will continue as a switch-hitter for the rest of the season to determine if it will be a wise procedure to follow next year."[21] Trosky told the writers that he felt "free and natural" from the right side. "Sure I'll keep on switching. Maybe if I had done it all season I would be fighting Joe [Vosmik]" for the batting title.[22]

On September 21, Trosky—who had returned to the left side of the plate, despite his earlier comments—hit his 24th home run of the year, this off White Sox ace Ted Lyons in a 7–3 Cleveland win, and he notched number 25 three days later in a 14–7 win over Detroit at League Park. His final homer of the blighted sophomore season came on the final Saturday of the year against the St. Louis Browns.

The long season closed with Trosky again driving in over 100 runs, finishing fourth in the league in that department behind Greenberg (with an amazing 170 RBI), Gehrig and Foxx. Trosky also finished fifth in the home run race with 26, but more importantly, by the end of the campaign had regained his rookie season swing. An almost 60-point drop in his batting average over his rookie numbers, and the commensurate drop in home runs, marred the season, but it proved to be useful preparation for the next season. "Trosky, when all is said and done, still is something more than a good gamble. He finished the season in a manner resembling his 1934 ... after a long slump, in which he tried every trick of stance except upside down."[23]

Rick Ferrell, echoing the wisdom of the baseball ages, observed that "A truly good hitter can adjust—there is no 'one way' to pitch to any good hitter. Any decent batter can adjust if you always throw, say, low and away."[24] Trosky did that. The 1935 season forced the 22-year-old Trosky to deal with longer-term failure and to return to the fundamentals of hitting. In many ways, the successes of 1936 would not have been possible without the trials and tribulations, and the subsequent adjustments, of 1935.

"Hal Trosky will be at first base for the Cleveland Indians next season" was Ed Bang's lead in an article in *The Sporting News* in October.[25] The subtext of the article was that, while Jimmie Foxx might be available at the right price, Alva Bradley and Cy Slapnicka were still pleased with Trosky. Bang dissected Trosky's season of slumps, recounting all of the physical remedies the hitter had tried, and speculated that the Walter Johnson conflict was more damaging than Trosky might have let on. "Trosky," he wrote, "is one of those sensitive boys who are heavily affected by environment."[26] The bottom line was that the press, the ownership, and presumably the ticket-buying public were willing to write off the year in the hope of a rebound in 1936.

In the front office, Alva Bradley elected to retain O'Neill as manager. Just about every newspaper labeled Trosky a "big disappointment" but they also acknowledged that a return to form in 1936 would put Cleveland right back into contention with Detroit and New York. Mel Harder won 20 games and Hudlin 15, while Thornton Lee provided a potentially reliable left-hander in a decent pitching rotation. In short, the public face of the team was one of optimism.

Further off the field, in the smoky backrooms of the team offices, the Indians' internal angst bubbled over in the off-season. In late November, after being asked to take a substantial pay cut[27] (since the team wasn't terribly profitable), general manager Billy Evans resigned—to be hired immediately by the Red Sox as farm director, and ultimately by the rival Tigers as GM. In Cleveland, Bradley terminated the office of "GM," instead naming Cy Slapnicka "assistant to the president," with orders to make the Indians respectable.

That would prove to be easier said than done.

◆ 5 ◆

At the Apex

Hal Trosky? He was a very nice man, very quiet. I don't know about him being that good a poker player. We'd ride all night on those trains between cities and get hot and sweaty and dirty. Wasn't much else to do but play cards but after everyone added up what they won and lost, I don't think anyone won or lost too much. It just helped the time go by.

—Willis Hudlin[1]

The winter following the 1935 season brought happy news. Despite his slight decline in overall batting production the previous season, Trosky earned a salary raise to $7,500 per year, roughly the equivalent of $125,000 in 2015 dollars.[2] The promotion of Cy Slapnicka, his principal advocate within the organization, to de facto general manager doubtless had some influence on this, but on a wider scale the larger national economy was also showing some signs, albeit spasmodic ones, of improvement. The Indians had a pretty clear idea of the value of the young man in relation to the team's future prospects.

The extra money came in handy in the Trosky household. By the start of spring training, Lorraine announced that she was pregnant with their first child. Hal's health had improved as well. After recurring stomach trouble throughout the 1935 season, he finally consulted with several doctors. The upshot was that he had developed an ulcer, probably due to stress. Regardless, with a new diet—which he followed to the letter—the ulcer had healed over. It was time to get back to the game.

Although life on the home front flowed smoothly, Trosky's baseball play during the pre-season in New Orleans was wretched. Picking up, or dropping off, in mid–1935 form, he rapped out only five hits in 27 at-bats early in the exhibition schedule. Unlike the previous season, though, this time he took it all in stride. To the press and to his team-mates, Trosky was far more mature than had been the awkward farm boy of two years earlier. No matter how poorly he performed at the plate, he made it a point not to over-react in the locker room or with the press. He also announced that he was abandoning the technique—born of desperation—of switch-hitting and was returning full-time to the left side of the plate. He told Ed McAuley,

> I'll do no right-handed batting this season. I know I switched last year, and with pretty good results, but if someone had told me at that time I might have hit better if I stood on my head I believe I'd have tried it. When the season was over and all the returns in, I found I had led the club and was near the top of the league in driving in runs. If I can do that in a season-long slump, there can't be so very much wrong with my batting style.[3]

The logic was sound. Trosky had again spent the off-season farming and playing basketball—the latter a fairly popular off-season conditioner among the younger major leaguers, having been used by players even since the days of Honus Wagner (himself an avid player)—so, when he reported to spring training at a muscular 208 pounds, Trosky was as lean as he'd been since turning professional.

Ticket sales were brisk as the Indians headed north after spring training. The 1934 "baby infield" was now two years older. Ed Bang noted that Walter Johnson was probably taking some satisfaction in knowing that the young cadre he'd assembled in 1935 was the same that Steve O'Neill proposed for 1936.[4] Additionally, star pitcher Johnny Allen had come over from the Yankees in an off-season trade for Monte Pearson and Steve Sundra. With Averill and Vosmik still patrolling the outfield, optimism was again the spirit of the day. Lorraine moved the family into the Shaker Heights neighborhood, in a mid-sized home on Riedham Road, and Trosky and neighbor Billy Sullivan would carpool the seven miles to the park for home games. Due to all of that quality time in the car, Sullivan in many ways probably knew Trosky as well as any of his teammates.

Sullivan, incidentally, was the son of catcher Billy Sullivan, Sr., the catcher for the 1906 "Hitless Wonders." That team earned the nickname because they finished that regular season with a league-low .230 team batting average and hit only seven homers the entire year, yet somehow managed to snatch the World Series from a Cubs team that had won 116 regular season games. Sullivan's son, Indians catcher William Jr., graduated from Notre Dame and played with the White Sox and the Cincinnati Reds before joining the Tribe in 1936. The younger Sullivan eventually played with seven teams in a 12-year career, but this season he hit .351 as an uber-utilityman for the Tribe, working behind the plate and playing both infield and outfield.

The season opened at League Park on Tuesday, April 14, with Cleveland mayor Harold H. Burton throwing out the first ball in front of about 18,000 fans, and with luminaries that included boxer Joe Louis and comedian Jack Benny in attendance.[5] The first Cleveland lineup of the year had the double play combination of shortstop Bill Knicker-bocker and Roy Hughes in the first two slots, followed by the big bats of Averill (CF), Vosmik (LF), Trosky in the fifth spot, and Bruce Campbell (RF) batting sixth. Catcher Frankie Pytlak, third baseman Boze Berger, and pitcher Mel Harder filled in the bottom three positions.

Joe Vosmik was an interesting cog in the Cleveland machine. He was a true native son, born in Cleveland, and had grown up with a slight obsession with baseball. He began playing for local teams as a teenager and, after being spotted by the Indians, signed with the team in 1928. In his rookie season, 1931, he hit .320 with 14 triples, 36 doubles, and 117 RBI, and during the 1935 campaign it was Vosmik and Averill who kept the offense afloat. Vosmik finished third in MVP voting that year while leading the American League in hits, doubles, and triples. However, 1936 would be his last with the Indians, as his batting average dropped from .348 to .287. He finished his career with a series of stops in St. Louis, Boston, Brooklyn, and Washington, but Cleveland was always home.

Talented as they were, though, the Indians faced a Tigers team that included five future Hall of Famers in Mickey Cochrane, Charlie Gehringer (called "The Mechanical Man," at second base), Hank Greenberg, Al Simmons, and Goose Goslin. In that season opener, Detroit's starting pitcher, Lynwood "Schoolboy" Rowe, allowed Cleveland only four hits as the defending World Series champion Tigers won, 3–0, at League Park. Trosky's day was anemic at best, taking a called strike three in the second inning and following that with a two groundouts to second and a foul pop fly to third baseman Marv Owen. The 0-for-4 performance by Trosky proved to be one of the few good deeds that the first baseman did for American League pitchers that year, as the next day the "1934" Hal Trosky model returned and smashed one of curveballer Tommy Bridges' offerings onto Lexington Avenue. For his 1936 encore, Trosky drove in four runs with the homer and two crisp singles on the day.

The following day, he pushed home Averill and Vosmik with a blast that reached the pavilion roof in St. Louis, while logging five RBI. The St. Louis hits were especially impressive because Trosky's right ankle was badly swollen and discolored after he accidently used the joint to stop a low line drive off the bat of Beau Bell in the first inning. Trosky didn't even take a day off. By April 20 he had logged his third homer in six games, and by the end of April a formidable Indians lineup was taking the field each day.

Bruce Campbell appeared to have recovered completely from a lingering case of meningitis, first contracted in St. Louis in 1934, and which at the time had been so debilitating that Browns manager Rogers Hornsby had finally given up and traded the promising hitter to Cleveland for Johnny Burnett and Bob Weiland. Averill and Vosmik were abusing enemy pitchers, and the Harder/Allen tandem was the foundation of a solid rotation.

On April 28, with the Yankees, Red Sox, Tigers, and Indians all playing at a .600 or better clip, Steve O'Neill bragged that his squad would be "in front or thereabouts right through the stretch." Just as quickly, though, Yankees pitchers took the measure of the Tribe and brought them back to reality. Red Ruffing shut them out, 2–0, Lefty Gomez beat them, 6–1 (and inspired one pundit to scrawl the obscure, and marginally racist, verse: "There's no hope. Injuns, when I whiz 'em. It's what they call 'Gomezmerism.'"[6]), and Monte Pearson beat the pitcher for whom he was traded, Johnny Allen, 8–1. Trosky made two errors in three games, but the Indians would have likely lost all three contests regardless.

In early May, another obstacle arose in Cleveland's quest. Slugging right fielder Bruce Campbell was stricken with a relapse of his meningitis on the train trip from New York and was admitted to the hospital as soon as the team arrived in Boston. The onset was initially mild, with Campbell merely complaining of minor cold symptoms. Those quickly gave way to a series of severe headaches, and Campbell's debilitation led the team to seek medical attention. Campbell's attending physician, Dr. William O'Halloran, told Gordon Cobbledick that meningitis was confirmed after a spinal fluid test and, given the player's history with the condition, his mother was brought to his bedside from her home in Cleveland.[7] With young Jim Gleeson filling in for Campbell in the outfield, though, the Indians went on a mini-tear, winning six in a row and nine of 12 before regressing to their mean.

The hospital stay left Trosky as the primary power source for the team. Along with his size, though, Trosky possessed great baseball instincts, and he used that guile to execute a rare steal of home in a late May contest against Washington. In the second inning, he singled off Jimmy Deshong and went to third on a Billy Sullivan single. Steve O'Neill ordered a double steal and at the pitch, Sullivan dutifully took off for second, where he barely eluded catcher Wally Millies' throw. A split-second later Trosky slid safely home, out of reach of Buddy Myers' off-line return peg. Despite the aggressiveness, the Indians lost that game, 7–6. On the positive side, Bruce Campbell sent a telegram to the team in late May stating, *"Please do not put me on the retired list. Will be ready in three weeks. Everything is all right."*[8] In other words, Campbell was pleading with Slapnicka and Bradley not to give up on him. Any job in the mid–1930s was a prize, and retaining one that involved playing major league baseball was worth every ounce of anxiety.

June also proved to be a tough month for Trosky. He was hospitalized as a result of a clot in his leg which developed following a batting practice accident in which he drove a pitch directly off his shin. After surgery to remove the clot on June 15, he missed only three games. On his first day back from the hospital, against an extraordinarily talented Yankees team that was embarking on four consecutive years of baseball domination, Trosky belted two home runs in a 6–5 Cleveland loss.

Adding injury to further injury, he was also hurt in a freakish play against the Red Sox. In the fifth inning at Fenway Park, he tripped over the feet of Boston coach Herb Pennock while moving into foul territory behind first base to catch a pop-up by pitcher Jim Henry. While Trosky lay on the ground, the ball (in classic cartoon fashion) continued downward and hit him squarely in the ear. The umpire charged Pennock with interference, so at least Trosky was credited with a putout for his sacrifice.

And for the loss of dignity.

The team as a whole was not immune to public insult, either. In a late-June *Sporting News* piece, the subtitle read: "Injury Jinx Does

Not Even Swing Sympathy of Clevelanders."[9] The criticism was reasonable, as the team hovered at just above .500 and appeared unable to gain any ground on the Yankees. Given the amount of pre-season hyperbole in the press, it was not surprising that the ticket-buying population was feeling underwhelmed by the team's performance. That is not to say that the team was failing. Cy Slapnicka told Ed McAuley that "I still say we have a good ball club, but too many of our players excel only mechanically. We need someone with fire and dash to serve as a spark plug."[10] The context of the quote was that the writer was profiling a young player named Roy "Stormy" Weatherly, but he was actually writing an apologia for the Indians' season to date.

Despite the team's collective performance, Trosky continued to punish American League pitching. By July 2, he had smote his 20th home run and had driven in 63 runs, virtually compelling both fans and press to forgive any perceived defensive flaws in his game. Gehrig and Foxx represented the American League at first base in the All-Star Game. That Trosky wasn't chosen for the team, despite his strong first-half performance, was understandable, especially in light of the super-human status of Gehrig and Foxx. To Trosky, it didn't matter, at least externally, as the break gave him an extra day at home with Lorraine.

Lou Gehrig is one of the best known names from baseball's past, but the array of first basemen playing in the American League during the Depression remains one of the greatest collections ever. Jimmie Foxx, aka "Double X" or "the Beast," was a prodigious slugger, strong enough to hold second place on the career home run list—behind Ruth—until 1966. He was not just a well-muscled power hitter, either. He won the American League Triple Crown in 1932, and his lifetime batting average of .325 accompanies 534 career homers, the latter mark still good enough for 18th place on the all-time list.

Despite his reputation as a heavy drinker,[11] Foxx was widely regarded as an affable man, a true "good guy" in the game. Rick Ferrell told a story about a game in 1934, Foxx batting and Ferrell catching, in which he kept trying to distract the hitter by engaging in friendly conversation. The first two times up, the normally talkative Foxx ignored Ferrell but produced just two, harmless fly outs. The third time up, after a couple of pitches, Foxx called for time, stepped out of the box, and told Ferrell to shut up. The two were friendly off the field, but Ferrell was under Foxx's skin. Ferrell smiled and said, "Sure, Jimmie."

Two of the finest first basemen in the American League during the 1930s: Hal Trosky and Jimmie Foxx. Foxx was simultaneously intimidating to opposing pitchers during the game, and equally gregarious off the diamond. Trosky regarded Foxx as one of the friendliest men he knew in baseball (Leslie Jones Collection, Boston Public Library).

As soon as he dropped back into his crouch, he started in again with "Didn't realize you were in such a bad mood. Everything OK at home?" Foxx evidently snorted and then laced a single to left. Ferrell laughed at the memory, but said he started right back in the next time the two met on the field.[12]

Trosky and Foxx were friendly on and off the field, although they did not have much opportunity to socialize. Trosky's son remembers that two of his father's best friends in baseball, who were not on the Indians, were Foxx and pitcher Lefty Gomez. Foxx passed away in 1967, but Trosky often hosted Gomez in Iowa whenever Gomez was in the area.

The Indians began the second half of 1936 in impressive fashion. Young phenom Bob Feller debuted on July 19, the day Trosky drove in his 90th run of the season, and by July 24 Cleveland had returned to second place. Quietly, Trosky put together a nice little hitting streak, which grew to 22 straight games by July 27 and began garnering attention in the sports pages outside of Ohio. On August 3, though, the streak finally stalled at 28 in a 9–4 loss to Detroit. Trosky's 28-game hitting streak was not just the longest such span in the major leagues in 1936, it remains the second-longest in Indians history.

It began innocently enough, as almost all such streaks do, on July 5, with a simple fourth-inning single in the first game of a doubleheader against Chicago. By the time the streak ended, it was the longest in team history, exceeded only by Sandy Alomar, Jr., in 1997, and Trosky's home-field consecutive game hit streak of 31 is still a team record. The streak represented the best month of Trosky's baseball life. In those 28 games, he came to bat 126 times and delivered 52 hits for a .413 batting average. Of those hits, 11 were home runs, and he drove in 38 runs. That pace, projected over a 154-game season, would have resulted in a Ruthian 60 homers and 209 RBI. Such was the magnitude of Trosky's streak, yet his streak was only half of what Joe DiMaggio would post a scant five years later. Regardless, he essentially carried the team for that period. By the end of July, he had slugged 30 home runs, many coming when the team needed it most, and the number of multiple-home run games nearly equaled his number of single-home run games, but nothing could ease the pressure applied by the Yankees.

Trosky's offensive production in mid–1936 buttressed a nine-game winning streak in the midst of a 19–8–1 stretch that elevated the Indians' record to 57–44. The tie came against the Yankees on August 3, in front of 65,342 fans on a Sunday afternoon at Cleveland Stadium, a game finally called at 4–4 due to darkness after 16 innings. At 7:15 p.m., after more than four hours of baseball, umpire George Moriarty finally declared the game over.

Inexorably, though, Cleveland began to slide in the standings. Fielding errors, rallies prematurely shortened, and uncharacteristically thin pitching mixed in various combinations to drag the Indians down. After a week with only one RBI, Trosky added some spice to the team's decline in a game against the White Sox at League Park in which he "connected for a solid line drive which traveled on a straight line to center, never varying its course so much as six inches [and] ... which rolled directly under the scoreboard"[13] off Ted Lyons. The shot required two relay throws just to get it back to the infield, by which time Trosky had crossed the plate. Such displays were a sideshow to the main event, the "Decline and Fall of the 1936 Indians."

On August 27, Trosky broke his own team record for home runs in a single season when he popped number 36 against the Senators. Cleveland maintained a hold on second place in the standings, but was still 14 games behind the Bronx Bombers. The movie "Last of the Mohicans" opened in theaters—quite appropriately—as the Red Sox cut the Indians' second-place margin to only one and a half games with Lefty Grove's seven-hitter on September 1. Two days later, the Yankees lit up Bob Feller for five first-inning runs and beat Cleveland, 6–4, and on September 6 the Tribe fell to fourth place.

Soon after, the rest of the 1936 season became a formality as the Yankees swept a League Park doubleheader to clinch the AL pennant. The Indians were not completely devastated, though, as Feller began to find his rhythm (highlighted by a 17-strikeout performance against the Athletics, one strikeout for each year of his life, on September 13). In the second game of the doubleheader against the A's, after Feller knifed through the Philadelphia lineup, Trosky hit his 38th home run of the season in his final at-bat. The next day he went 4-for-4 with two home runs and seven RBI. That performance put him back in the lead of the American League RBI race, ahead of Gehrig, and he added five more the next day with another 4–4 performance in support of Bill Zuber's winning effort.

Feller's story appears in an array of other books and encyclopedias, but he and Trosky enjoyed a friendly bond from the outset simply based on their shared Iowa heritage. Joining a big league team as a well-hyped teenage phenom was loaded with implied pressure. Joining a team mid-season, one that was supposed to have challenged the Yankees but was instead scrambling simply to remain in the first division, was worse. Trosky immediately took Feller under his wing,[14] not so much to keep him out of the spotlight, but to help the boy deal with the rougher reporters and the occasional irrationality of the paying public.

Bob Feller, of course, went on to post a 266–162 record and is on a short list of those considered the greatest right-handers of all time. He remains the Indians' career leader in shutouts, innings pitched, wins, and strikeouts (2,581). Feller appeared in eight All-Star Games, started two of them (1941 and 1946), won 20 games six times, and tossed three three no-hitters. All of these remarkable statistics accrued despite his missing 1942–1944 and most of 1945 while serving in the U.S. Navy.[15] Feller remained fond of Trosky and was protective of his friend's legacy. "They [the press] didn't really know what was going on [referring to a 1940 incident]. They just blamed Hal and Mel [Harder] and me because everyone knew who we were."[16]

Cleveland had dipped into fifth place, the distasteful "second division," for the first time on September 15. That would be their home for the rest of the season. The final standings placed the Indians 22½ games behind the Yankees and two out of the first division. The absence of guaranteed contracts made on-field performance the critical factor in determining salaries for the 1937 season, so the players certainly played with pressure. It was again fruitless, as the team played out the string in advance of yet another winter with no World Series.

On September 26, baseball momentarily lost relevance to Trosky as he and Lorraine welcomed their first child, a boy, into the world. He, too, would go on to achieve his own baseball success, but there will be more on that later. The family of three returned to Iowa in October for another winter of farming. After the success of the last season, spring training couldn't get there quickly enough. "Trosky last year," one article noted, "received a reported $7,500. After a season in which he ranked first in runs-batted-in, second in home runs, and was generally rated a player of the Gehrig and Foxx class, the big farm boy from Norway ... might easily be expected to have some fancy notions about the contract figure."[17]

The newsprint post mortems began rolling in in early October. The legal case surrounding the legality of Bob Feller's signing was the 800-pound gorilla in the room, but neither Bradley nor Slapnicka wished to try the case in the press. Ed Bang opined that Bradley would be doing some "important remodeling" over the winter, even if that amounted to no more than finding a few reinforcements for the existing lineup.[18] There were reports of various trade options to improve Cleveland's catching corps, but Bradley was hesitant to break up what he apparently thought was, at its core, a solid team.[19]

On balance, 1936 was a tough year for pitchers. The American League Earned Run Average was 5.04, due in some part to the presence of the best group of slugging first basemen ever assembled. Chicago shortstop Luke Appling paced all hitters with a .388 average, while Lou

Gehrig was fifth with a mark of .354. Trosky and Foxx were close behind at .343 and .338, respectively. In the power department, Gehrig led everyone with 49 home runs, followed by Trosky's 42 and Foxx's 41.

In RBI, Trosky posted what remains tied with Babe Ruth's 1931 campaign for the 19th-best single-season total (as of 2016) with 162, and he also racked up a league-leading 405 total bases. Gehrig trailed him in both categories, as did Foxx and big Zeke Bonura (of the White Sox) in RBI. Trosky's 405 total bases remain the 23rd-highest single-season total.[20]

Most impressively, the big Bohemian smote 96 extra-base hits, one of the 30 best seasons ever. Only Lou Gehrig, Hank Greenberg, Chuck Klein, Albert Belle, Todd Helton and the incomparable Ruth ever had more than one season with 96 or more extra-base hits, while Joe DiMaggio, Jimmie Foxx, Rogers Hornsby, and Trosky are among 15 sluggers who did it once each. Consider those excluded from that power club: Ted Williams never had 90 extra-base hits in a year; Mickey Mantle never had a season with 80; Mike Schmidt's highest output was 81, Willie Mays 90, and Hank Aaron 92. The club is exclusive, requiring both the ability to hit consistently and with power in order to qualify.

Detractors of Trosky's season have pointed out that 30 of his 42 home runs and 99 of his 162 RBI were cracked at League Park. The 290-foot foul line in

A more mature Trosky on the cusp of his 1936 season. Trosky led the American League with 162 RBI and 405 total bases, while competing against the likes of Lou Gehrig, Jimmie Foxx, Hank Greenberg and a rookie from San Francisco named Joe DiMaggio (*Cleveland Press Collection*, Michael Schwartz Library, Cleveland State University).

right field probably did account for some of his shots, but the 40-foot-high wall and abrupt opening to deep center field no doubt took some away. Society for American Baseball Research (SABR) member George Wiley, formerly a professor of history at Indiana University in Pennsylvania, undertook a statistical review of the 357 doubles the Indians hit in 1936 in order to judge the effect of the right field wall on the team's slugging.[21] Wiley found that 209 of the 357 team doubles were hit at League Park, and 35 percent of those finding the right field wall. Of Trosky's 45 doubles, just over half (27) were hit at League Park that year, and only eight "ricocheted" off the wall. Not to dismiss the math, but to assume that power numbers derived exclusively from ballpark geometry is to undersell what was, in reality, a potent Cleveland attack.

Trosky was the sort of hitter who frequently lofted high and long fly balls as a product of a slight upward arc in his swing; since he was basically a left-handed "dead pull hitter" that year, any park's right field wall would have been an inviting target. A ball leaving League Park, even at the 290-foot mark, had to climb over 40 feet in the air. The extra distance acquired on a descent would have carried even those "short shots" out of many other ball parks in the major leagues. Penalizing Trosky for hitting in League Park simultaneously diminishes the achievements of Ruth and Gehrig, left-handed hitters in a stadium with an almost equally short (296 foot) right field line and a much lower fence at the end of that line.

Wiley wrote, "It is more than coincidence that the New York Yankees, who hit 15 of their 16 home runs in Cleveland over the wall, also had a short right field fence back home. The Boston Red Sox, whose own inviting wall was in left field, hit only four home runs in League Park [that year]."[22] Successful teams have always built their rosters and lineups based, at least in part, on ballpark geometry. It just makes sense.

◈ **6** ◈

Years of Stability

I first met Hal in 1933 and he was truly a great player. In my opinion, he was the best first baseman in Cleveland Indians' history. During the last few years of his career, Hal suffered from migraine headaches and I don't know how he made it through some games. He was a very good friend.

—Mel Harder[1]

Beemer, Nebraska's favorite son, Melvin Leroy "Chief" Harder, was an important friend and teammate to both Hal Trosky and Bob Feller, along with just about every pitcher who darkened the doorway of Cleveland's locker room between 1928 and 1963. His 20-year pitching career remains the longest in Indians history, and his subsequent tenure as pitching coach may be just as impressive.

As a player, Harder twice won 20 games and led the American League in ERA in 1933. Even more notable, however, was his performance in All-Star Games. He represented the Indians for four consecutive years, 1934–1937, and in that span put up a mark still unequalled in All-Star Game history. In the 1934 game, the second one ever held and forever remembered as the game in which Carl Hubbell fanned Ruth, Gehrig, Foxx, Simmons, and Joe Cronin consecutively, Harder relieved starter Red Ruffing in the middle of the fifth inning with the National League threatening to close the AL's 8–4 lead. He merely pitched the rest of the game, gave up no runs, and earned the win. In the 1935 game, he tossed three more shutout innings to preserve Lefty Gomez' win. In 1936 he threw two more shutout innings in closing the game, and in 1937 saved another game with three more innings of scoreless relief.

In all, Mel Harder's All-Star record includes a win, two retroactive saves, and 13 shutout innings against the best batters in the National

League. He is remembered, accurately, as one of the greatest Indians of all time, and Hal Trosky regarded him with greater respect than any other teammate in his career.[2]

With Adolf Hitler now more than a shadow on the horizon in Europe, and the Japanese sun rising in Asia, talk in the Cleveland clubhouse naturally began to drift to international events and the potential for war. Discussing those issues, along with the new baby in the Trosky house, probably had a way of keeping baseball in perspective. The Northern Ohio writers, however, did their best to try to accord sports a degree of over-importance.

From a Cleveland newspaper in early 1937:

> With all due respect to the manifest ability displayed by Ruth, Gehrig, and Simmons, the "long term" guys in punching in runs, there is one individual who casts a shadow over this great trio. I am referring to none other than the young man who cavorts around the first stopping place for the Indians. Yap [*sic*]. Hal Trosky, none other but. In his first three years under the big canvas, Trosky surpassed the efforts of the aforementioned big three in their "win, place, and show" seasons. Simmons exploded to the extent of 102, 129, and 109, for 340 markers. Gehrig's record was 350, made up of 68, 107, and 175. Ruth's added up to 403: 138, 170, and 96. As for Trosky, well, Hal started with 142, followed with 113 and rounded out his three years by leading both leagues in driving in runs last season with 162. Even the kids in first grade will tell you that makes 417, which takes the prize.

Rather than listen to the hype surrounding his previous three seasons, especially the monstrous 1936 campaign, Trosky approached 1937 with the focused intention of helping the Indians in the field. In his two biggest offensive years, 1934 and 1936, he led American League first basemen with 22 errors each season, and the stigma of being a slipshod defender nagged at his professional conscience.

The other area in which he was determined to improve was in drawing walks. Despite striking out only 167 times from 1934–1936, he felt that he needed to be even more selective at the plate. In 1936, he earned only 36 free passes, 22 fewer than in 1934, despite a high average and 103 home runs over the three seasons. Beyond that, though, it looked to be business as usual in 1937. Trosky remained the centerpiece of a potent Cleveland lineup that now included Lyn Lary at shortstop (replacing Bill Knickerbocker) and Julius "Moose" Solters in left field. The team had also added another Iowan, pitcher Earl Whitehill, in a three-way trade with the White Sox and the Senators.

The 1937 Cleveland Indians. Trosky is second from the left in the back row (*Cleveland Press* Collection, Michael Schwartz Library, Cleveland State University).

Earl Whitehill played 17 major league seasons and remains in the top 100 in wins. A southpaw, he mixed a tantalizing curve with a fiery disposition to win 218 games for the Detroit Tigers, Washington Senators, Cleveland Indians, and Chicago Cubs.

The son of Noah and Margaret Whitehill, Earl hailed from Cedar Rapids, Iowa, which he called home throughout his life. Born February 7, 1899, his height is listed in various places between 5'9½" to 5'10" with a weight of about 175 pounds, although his draft card from World War I declares him to be of medium height and slender build.

Discovered by fellow Cedar Rapids native Cy Slapnicka, who scouted for the Tigers before moving to Cleveland, Whitehill began ascending the ziggurat of organized baseball at age 20, playing two games at Des Moines in 1919. In 1920, he went 20–10 at Columbia before reporting to Birmingham late in the season. He stayed with Birmingham from 1921 through 1923 and finally reported to Detroit in late 1923.

He won 74 games in four minor league seasons. Clearly ready for the big time, Detroit purchased his contract from Birmingham and brought him up to play for manager Ty Cobb late in 1923. He made his first appearance on September 15, at age 24, and logged 33 innings over eight games while garnering a 2–0 record. In 1924, Whitehill became a Tigers starter, replacing 34-year-old Hooks Dauss, and validated Cobb's judgment that season by leading all AL rookies with 17 wins and a .654 winning percentage.

That year he also married 22-year-old Violet Oliver. There has persisted through the literature a popular "urban legend" that she was the original model for the Sun-Maid Raisins "maiden." The Sun-Maid Raisin Company has since publicly stated that Lorraine Collette Peterson was the actual model, and there is no record of Violet being painted or drawn for the role in 1916, when the image first adorned the raisin boxes. She was, regardless, a beautiful woman, and the couple doubtless drew attention wherever they went. Violet became close with Claire Ruth during the Connie Mack/Babe Ruth 1934 barnstorming tour of Japan, and the two couples were friendly off the field. Of course, the Bambino loved facing Whitehill on the field, too, as Ruth tagged him for 11 of his 714 career home runs (only six pitchers gave up more four-baggers to the Babe).

Over a ten-year span Whitehill posted a 133–120 record for the Tigers. Control was the primary feature of his game, and he used his array of off-speed pitches to win 14 or more games ten times, all too often for mediocre teams. On December 14, 1932, the Tigers traded Whitehill to Washington for pitchers Fred "Firpo" Marberry and Carl Fischer.

The 1933 season began in turmoil. In April, Whitehill hit Lou Gehrig—at the time closing in on Everett Scott's 1,308 consecutive-games-played record—and knocked him unconscious. Gehrig recovered, but Whitehill continued to finding himself in the midst of maelstroms.

In May, as part of an imbroglio between the Yankees' Ben Chapman and Senators shortstop Buddy Myer, Whitehill even achieved notoriety in the May 8, 1933, issue of *Time* magazine:

> When Chapman reached the passageway on his way off the field, Earl Whitehill, Washington pitcher, called him a bad name. This was more than Fielder Chapman, already humiliated, could bear. He rushed at Whitehill, hit him. Umpire Moriarty tried to pull the fighters apart but failed. This time, all the players on both teams rushed at each other not to stop the fight but to enlarge it. Private detectives, uniformed police officers and about 300 spectators rushed down on

the field. The spectators, armed with bats they had picked up, tried to bash the players. The players bashed each other and the spectators. After 20 minutes, police managed to restore enough order for the ball game to proceed. After five more innings, the Yankees won 16 to 0.

Although they weren't teammates for long, the hard-won wisdom and experience of Ty Cobb manifested themselves throughout White-hill's career. Chapman got a measure of revenge the next year, however, when he broke up Whitehill's potential no-hitter against the Yankees on May 30, 1934.

Whitehill led the AL in games started and was near the top in most pitching categories in 1933. That autumn he defeated Freddie Fitzsimmons of the Giants, 4–0, with at five-hitter in Game Three of the World Series.

As he had demonstrated earlier, his temper could be both fierce and short. He achieved the dubious "century mark" on the mound by hitting 101 batters over his career and is popularly regarded as a temperamental pitcher who often showed up in the top ten in hit batsmen. He led the league in that category in his first full year, 1924, when he hit 13 (tied with George Uhle). In pitcher Elden Auker's memoir, *Sleeping Cars and Flannel Uniforms*, the former Tiger relates a story about a time he and Whitehill played golf in Arizona during spring training. Well down the fairway, a golf ball suddenly landed close to Whitehill, and he charged back to the tee box to "take care" of the hacker. Providentially, his fellow golfers talked him out of the quest, as later on they learned that the "assailant" was actually heavyweight champion Jack Dempsey.[3]

His temper notwithstanding, Whitehill had his best season in 1933, and his pitching was largely responsible for the Senators finding themselves in the World Series against the Giants. New York enjoyed a 2–0 Series lead when Whitehill took the hill for the third game. He made the most of his only World Series appearance by tossing a complete game shutout of the Giants, scattering five hits and two walks in front of 25,727 spectators at Griffith Stadium. In doing so, he also held future Hall of Famers Mel Ott and Bill Terry to a collective 0-for-7 day at the plate. On the biggest stage, Whitehill brought his best stuff.

Whitehill pitched three more consistent, winning seasons for Washington, despite one aberrant game in 1935 in which he gave up ten doubles, but on December 10, 1936, he anchored the three-team trade that sent him to Cleveland. The Senators received Jack Salveson from the White Sox, while Chicago got Thornton "Lefty" Lee from the Indians.

In Cleveland, Whitehill appeared more often in relief. He won 17 games and lost 16 for the Indians in the 1937–1938 seasons, and in February 1939 was released. The Chicago Cubs signed him for the 1939 season, and he finished that year, the last of his career, with a 4–7 record. By the end of his career he was the oldest player in the National League. His final game came on September 30, 1939.

The Indians hired him as a coach after the 1940 season, but let him go in November 1941. Whitehill's final stop in the majors, after a season in the International League, was as coach of the Philadelphia Phillies in 1943. After that, he took up traveling sales of sporting goods, using his name to represent the A.G. Spalding Company.

His lifetime record compares well with luminaries such as Bob Feller and Red Faber. Feller appeared in 570 games and won 266; Faber in 662 games, winning 254; Whitehill pitched in 541 games, won 218 against 185 losses, and amassed 3,564⅔ innings of big league baseball. Unquestionably durable, he tossed 226 complete games and walked only 1,431 batters. On the not-so-good side, he was not a deft fielder, twice committing seven errors in a single season. He was inducted into the *Des Moines Register*'s Iowa Sports Hall of Fame in March 1963. None other than "Cool Papa" Bell, the Negro Leagues legend, noted in an American Heritage interview with John Holway that "Earl Whitehill was the toughest big-league pitcher I ever faced. In 1929 we beat the major-league all-stars six out of eight games, and Whitehill beat us both times."

In late 1954, at an intersection in Omaha, Nebraska, a car flew through a stop sign and t-boned Whitehill's car. Though shaken, he refused to go to the hospital on the night he was injured. The next day, however, he was forced to visit a doctor, and the medical team discovered that the pitcher had suffered a fractured skull. Whitehill lived for another week but passed away on October 22. He is buried at Cedar Memorial Park, near his former home.

Cy Slapnicka had endured a busy winter, traveling to the homes of various players to negotiate contracts for the upcoming season. Remember, this was a time in which players were contracted year-to-year, with no security for the future, yet still bound to their clubs by the notorious "reserve clause." The teams held all the power. That position wasn't forcibly challenged until Marvin Miller came along in the 1960s and 1970s, and it was generally accepted as a condition of employment when Trosky played. Of course, with the Great Depression still sucking the energy out of the economy, players in the 1930s were simply pleased to have jobs.

That stipulated, annual salary negotiations could occasionally become contentious, especially if player and team (in a time before agents) disagreed on the value of the player's contributions. So Slapnicka hit the road to get his roster under contract before they were to report to New Orleans. Feller, still in school, was given a raise to $10,000 per year, and Slapnicka reached agreements with Vosmik and Harder fairly quickly as well. Trosky, as expected following his monster 1936 season, nearly doubled his salary. The 24-year-old slugger would earn $13,500, a $6,000 raise on his 1936 compensation, for the coming campaign.

"The most encouraging feature," wrote Ed McAuley of the young pre-season, "has been the Indians' batting power.... Hal Trosky and Earl Averill are hitting home runs almost everywhere they go."[4] As they had since 1934, the New York Giants and the Indians paired up for a pre-season slate of games, barnstorming through Mississippi, Louisiana, Oklahoma, Arkansas, Georgia and the Carolinas, a plan that gave fans throughout the southern and western states the opportunity to see star players like Feller, Carl Hubbell, and Earl Averill in relatively intimate settings. The scheme also gave the Indians the chance to do their spring work against what would prove to be the best team in the National League that year.

One exhibition series in Oklahoma gave baseball fans in the western United States their first chance to see Trosky hit as well. Over 5,000 locals wedged into the Shawnee, Oklahoma, minor league park on April 8 to see nearby Meeker, Oklahoma's favorite son, Carl Hubbell, take the hill for the New York Giants. In the midst of what the papers termed a "raging dust storm" (this was the tail end of the dust-bowl maelstrom), though, Trosky launched one of Hubbell's screwballs into the outfield bleachers. Hubbell won the war, allowing only two hits and one run, while striking out four in three innings of work, but the Cleveland slugger showed every indication of picking up where he had left off the previous season.

6. Years of Stability

"Any manager who predicts where his team will finish is simply silly, isn't he?"[5] That quote, from Steve O'Neill, came from the bedside of pitcher Johnny Allen, who had been admitted to a St. Louis hospital for an appendectomy on May 1. Some of the local writers were again beginning to circle like wolves around potential prey, more frequently questioning O'Neill's capability as skipper. Regardless, the team was four games over .500, at 18–14, on June 1.

Earlier in May, Trosky became the first player ever to hit two home runs in a game at Cleveland's Municipal Stadium, a venue used more frequently in the latter part of the decade. On May 26, Billy Sullivan and Bruce Campbell both hit pinch-homers, the first time that had ever occurred in an American League game, and the heroics led to a Tribe win. But the spasms of production did not routinely translate into wins on the field. From June 15–27, the Tribe suffered through a disastrous 12-game road trip, winning exactly twice. Then panic set in.

Gone was the easy-going, "players' manager" version of Steve O'Neill, replaced in the dugout by an increasingly desperate alter-ego that banned poker and late sleeping until they started winning. Specifically, he directed that all players be up by 9 a.m. and have finished breakfast by 10 a.m. He even required players to mark their "breakfast time on their checks as they sign them."[6] It was an odd remedy, in that O'Neill didn't ban card games like bridge or even blackjack. Only poker, he said, because "aside from the money involved, [it] develops an intense interest—and our only interest right now is in winning games."[7]

On June 30, Trosky had yet another two-homer game against St. Louis, and on July 5 found more "doubleheader magic." In the first game of the twin bill against the Browns, facing former teammate Oral Hildebrand and a roster that included Tribe alumni Joe Vosmik and Bill Knickerbocker, he flied out to right field in his first at-bat, stranding Roy Hughes at second. In the fourth he managed a single, but again failed to cross home plate. In the fifth inning, however, the floodgates finally burst. Trosky hit a three-run shot and followed that up with a solo blast in the seventh. In the eighth frame, now facing Sheriff Blake, Trosky hit another three-run bomb for his third homer of the game. He came to bat again in the ninth, but struck out with Averill on second.[8] On the day, Trosky smote three consecutive home runs and drove in seven runs in a 14–4 Cleveland romp. In the second game, he drove in one more run to bring his tally to eight for the day. As a side-note, the total time for both games, in which 37 runs scored, was only four hours and 32 minutes.

Trosky hit four homers in a three games in Detroit a few days later and raised his batting average to .296. By July 18, the average was up to .302, and even the national press was noticing the improvement in his defense. "Trosky has worked doggedly to improve his defensive play. Actually, he is something like 300 per cent better than he was ... in 1933."[9] Still, the team fell to five games below .500 after being swept in a four-game set in Boston early in August, and the cries for O'Neill's job were everywhere. Injuries were part of the problem, but every team suffers injuries. Trosky took two days off due to a hand injury sustained from mishandling a throw from Lyn Lary, and he was joined on the shelf by Johnny Allen (appendicitis), Feller (arm soreness), Billy Sullivan (split finger), John Kroner (hives), Lloyd Brown (sinus), Roy Hughes (split between the fingers on his right hand), and Roy Weatherly (the deliberately vague diagnosis of "soreness").

O'Neill's real problem lay 450 miles to the east, in New York. The Indians finished the 1937 season with a winning record, thanks in large part to 23 September wins. That they were a winning team but still 19 games behind the Yankees is as much an endorsement of the team in the Bronx as a critique of any failings in Cleveland.

Much of the public attention on the Indians in 1937 focused on pitcher Johnny Allen's bid to break the league record for consecutive victories. On September 21 against the Senators, Trosky contributed a rare inside-the-park, grand slam home run—on a line drive misjudged by outfielder Mel Almada—that aided Allen in his 13th straight win in the 6–3 Indians victory. On October 2, he hit home runs number 31 and 32 against the Tigers, and the next day Allen took the hill in pursuit of a perfect 16–0 record. The drama lured over 20,000 fans to the corner of Michigan and Trumbull in Detroit, despite the fact that the Yankees had already secured their second consecutive World Series bid, to see Allen battle Tigers pitcher Jake Wade. Wade had a losing record for the season, but Hank Greenberg put the Tigers ahead early with his 183rd RBI of the season, and Wade proved up to the challenge.

Trosky had the only Cleveland hit of the day, a single in the seventh inning, and had a chance to be a hero when he came to bat in the ninth inning with two outs. Lyn Lary had walked and was sacrificed to second,

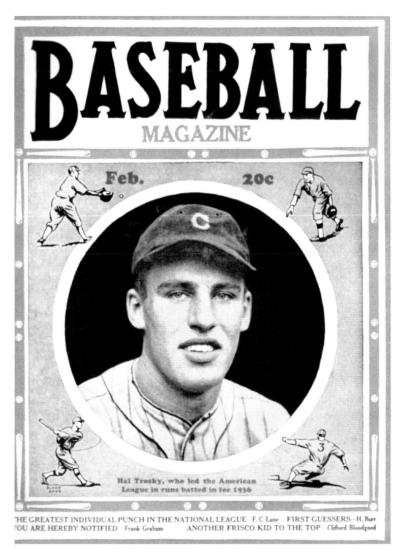

Trosky graced the cover of *Baseball Magazine* in February 1937. With spring training only a month away, the journal highlighted the biggest slugging star of 1936. In that era, *Baseball Magazine* and *The Sporting News* were the two primary media for fans. The magazine went out of business in the early 1950s.

but the first baseman struck out swinging to end the game. Despite allowing only one run on five Detroit hits, Allen's streak ended.

Allen was perhaps the only player on the team in Whitehill's class of orneriness. The North Carolina native had exploded onto the American

League in 1932, posting a 17–4 mark with the Yankees and following that up in 1933 with a 15–7 record. Lou Gehrig was widely quoted as saying that "(Allen) thinks he should win every time he pitches, and that if he loses it's a personal conspiracy against him." In 1935, after one particularly tough loss, Allen took Yankees manager Joe McCarthy to task. The tantrum didn't improve Allen's result, but it did convince the Yankees to trade their talented pitcher to the Indians for pitchers Monte Pearson and Steve Sundra that December.

Allen led the Tribe with 20 wins in 1936, and despite a few of his patented, high-profile rage episodes after some of the losses, he proved to be a legitimate frontline starter for the team in 1937. He went on to win 12 straight decisions in 1938, but irreparably hurt his arm in the All-Star Game that year. By 1940 he was barely better than a .500 pitcher, and the Indians sold him to the Browns for a reported $20,000. Allen kicked around with various teams through 1944 before his final release from baseball.

For Trosky, despite finishing just two hits south of a .300 batting average in 1937, his 32 home runs were the sixth-best mark in the American League, and he finished fifth in the RBI race with 128. In all, the team did deceptively well at 83–71, but the Yankees dynasty refused to lose.

Refreshingly, Trosky was no longer the "Iron Glove" of the American League, as he passed that mantle to Lou Gehrig, the former making ten errors compared to the latter's 16. Never again would Trosky commit more than 11 errors in a season or lead the league in that most dubious category. In an "unofficial" tribute to the success the young man was enjoying, despite his inability to crack the American League All-Star team lineup, he was chosen to grace the front of a "Wheaties" cereal box. There were six cover boys in 1937, including Earl Averill, Lefty Gomez, Bronko Nagurski, Mel Ott, and Cecil Travis. Lofty company indeed.

Upon Trosky's return to Iowa for the off-season, Norway staged a "Hal Trosky Day" baseball game in his honor. According to local Iowa writer and baseball historian Cliff Trumpold, "Red" Hibben pitched for Norway against the rival town team from Van Horne. The latter, in a legitimate effort to win the game, brought in Amana native and Trosky's Cleveland teammate, fastballer Bill Zuber, just in time to face Norway on his friend's big day. Zuber won.

1938

The big news for the Indians over the off-season came in the form of a new manager: Oscar Vitt replaced Steve O'Neill. O'Neill was, with a few exceptions, gregarious, popular with the players, self-confident, and straightforward. "Ole Os" Vitt, as some reporters referred to him, was not.

Formerly a defensive specialist for the Tigers of Ty Cobb's era, yet a player who could barely hit his weight, Vitt had managed the minor league Newark Bears to the AAA minor league championship the year before. Many baseball insiders said—only half in jest—that the Yankees' farm club was the second-best team in baseball. In Cleveland, part of the uncertainty surrounding Vitt was that the Bears had so much talent that he, as manager, could virtually sit back, roll out a baseball, and watch his players dominate the opposition. At least that was the mumbling from the loyal backers of the ousted O'Neill.

Vitt did not exactly endear himself to his new players. Immediately after taking over, "Ole Os" made a public pronouncement that he "had only two major leaguers, Feller and Harder." In his first public pronouncement, he told the press that he planned to make the players walk the two miles from Heinemann Park, their training site in New Orleans, to their downtown hotel after every practice.[10] Alva Bradley, in hiring Vitt, also ceded trade authority to his new manager. The second-order effect of that arrangement was to create immediate, implicit tension between Vitt and Slapnicka.

The Sporting News ran a story identifying the various power centers in Bradley's organization. Organizationally, the story implied, there was no clear leadership structure.[11] Team general counsel Joseph Hostetler, road secretary Frank Kohlbecker, Bradley, Vitt and Slapnicka formed an odd hierarchy, actually more of a flat organization, and in retrospect, it is clearer why the team struggled during Vitt's tenure.

One undeniable truth about Oscar Vitt, however, was that he cared about winning baseball games more than just about anything else in his professional world. People and their feelings were of less consequence to Vitt than winning. As one example: In a pre-season exhibition on April 6, in Longview, Texas, a community in the easternmost part of the state, an estimated 5,000 fans jammed the local park, with an estimated capacity of 3,000, to watch the Giants and Indians play.

Left to right: Trosky, Oscar Vitt and Bob Feller on the top step of the dugout in 1938. Those were happier times, before the disaster of 1940 (Leslie Jones Collection, Boston Public Library).

Umpire Claude Tobin, traveling with the teams, went over the ground rules before the game and reminded both managers that any ball hit into the overflowing crowd would be ruled a double and the ball would be dead.

Tied 4–4 in the ninth inning, Joe Moore tagged a pitch into the part of the crowd that had overflowed into fair territory. Cleveland's Moose Solters raced after the ball and made a terrific catch in the crowd, which created a dilemma for Tobin. Following his initial impulse, the umpire raised his fist and called Moore out. After consultation with the other umpire, Lou Kolls, though, Tobin changed his mind and ruled Moore safe at second. Vitt flipped out. According to one report, "The crowd took sides. Arguments ensued. Punches were thrown. Hundreds of fans left the grandstand and swarmed the field."[12] Vitt pulled his team off the diamond and left the facility. The story became national news when commissioner Kenesaw Mountain Landis fined Vitt $200 for the incident.[13]

Vitt, however, quickly proved that he did actually know a thing or two about baseball once the new and improved Trosky was unveiled. In a mid–March exhibition against the Phillies in New Orleans, Vitt "was shocked to learn that the Tribe's opponents were playing Hal Trosky as a batter who couldn't send a ball to the left side of second base if he aimed it with a cannon."[14] In what was actually an old tactic against left-handed pull hitters, opponents often shifted most of their infield to the right side of second base, essentially daring Trosky—or any dead pull hitter—to go to the opposite field. The tactic has stimulated all sorts of discussion in recent seasons, as the old tactic became the new tactic[15] even though it has been around for generations. Regardless, Vitt was not pleased. "In 29 years in baseball I've never seen such a thing. Why it's brutal. It's insane. It can't be. We've got to make him hit to left."[16]

"From now on," Vitt told *The Sporting News* a week later,

> Trosky will be trying to hit to left field every time up. Why, just think of the advantage he will have if he can poke even one hit a game down that third base line. Not only will his average go up 50 or 60 points, but he'll force those infields to play normally for him, and then he'll have so much better a chance to rifle those power drives down the right side. I don't believe in ruining a good hitter in the effort to make him a better one, but during the spring games, at least, Trosky will be aiming toward left. If I see he simply can't master the trick, I'll just have to let him swing for right field, but his value will be greatly increased if he can learn to cross up those unorthodox infield settings.[17]

Bob Kennedy, the former player and manager, said of Trosky: "You couldn't make a mistake on him. Of course he played in that bandbox, League Park, which made him all the more dangerous. He stood on top of the plate and pulled everything."[18] Vitt convinced him to stop swinging for the fences and just use his superior vision and plate discipline to drive the ball to the opposite field. Vitt's plan bore immediate fruit. On March 16 Trosky slammed a single, double, and triple to left or left-center field against the Phillies, delighting both player and manager. By the end of March, after a three-hit game in Chicago which included a double to the left field corner and two singles to the left side of second base, the fielding shift against the slugger quickly disappeared.

The manager wasn't an absolutist about the change, noting that "in League Park he can hit to right as much as he wants to. That's his percentage, with that wall to shoot at. But learning to hit to left ought to double his batting average on the road."[19] "I've forgotten all that home run stuff," Trosky told Ed McAuley, "though I imagine on sheer power I'll get at least 25 this season. In the past, I was always trying to pull the ball. No batter living can consistently pull outside pitches."[20] After 20 games, Trosky was cruising, batting at a .415 clip, and he finally developed some confidence in his fielding. While his range around the base was limited by his relatively large size, he now had four years of experience and had developed the soft hands needed to handle all the types of throws which came his way from the other infielders.

In an interview with Frank Gibbons, he talked about how he handled the position.

> I had played first base just about six weeks when the Indians got me. Sure, I've learned a few things about playing the bag. I'm no Hal Chase, but I'm not a clothing store dummy, either.... I don't advise stretching for all throws. One of the things you get used to doing is deciding whether to stretch or not. If it's a well-hit ball, fielded cleanly, there's no reason for stretching. The ball might be thrown over your head. But when you see it's going to be off, stretch as far as you can.[21]

What did he think was the toughest fielding situation? Not surprisingly,

> "If he's a right handed thrower, like me, that double play from first to second and back is pretty tough. Most of the time you've got to throw over or to either side of the runner's head as he goes to second. I usually try to throw to the right side. That play from first baseman to pitcher on a ball hit deep to first isn't so tough to make. You just toss under handed, trying to time it with the pitcher's arrival at the bag. Sacrifice bunts are hard for a first baseman to play, too, unless he gets a little help from the infield. Suppose there's a man on first and the batter sacrifices to me. I've got to run in and grab the ball, size up the runner coming to first and turn and do the same thing to the runner going to second. If there's a chance of cutting off the runner going to second I throw there. Sometimes it might be too late. In these cases it's good to have another infielder, who has the play in front of him, calling out the proper base.[22]

It was obvious that Trosky had paid attention to Steve O'Neill's fielding instruction. He made only ten errors in 1938, contrasted with Foxx's league-leading 19, and when coupled with his new approach at the plate, had transitioned from "slugger" to "baseball player."

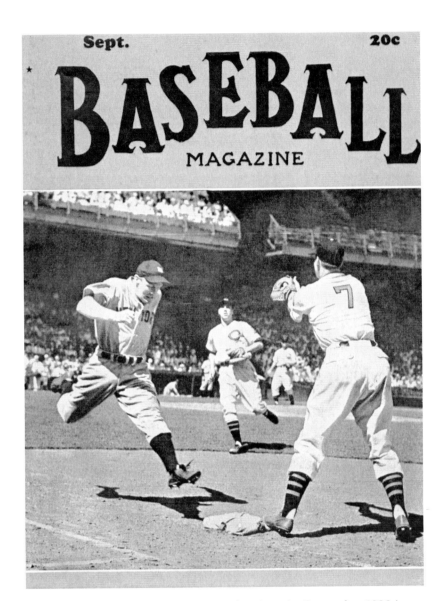

BASEBALL
MAGAZINE

Another cover of *Baseball Magazine*, this time the September 1938 issue, with Trosky taking a throw from Bob Feller to retire Red Rolfe of the New York Yankees.

By mid–May, Vitt's managerial style had become clear. He was unafraid to fine players, even his stars, for what he perceived as a lack of hustle. He benched one of his two best hitters in 1937, Moose Solters, for three games when the latter's average dipped below .150, and stuck

Roy Weatherly in left field as a replacement. The move was physically striking, as Solters was slightly more than 6' tall, while his replacement was listed as 5'6", and possibly smaller than that. Trosky didn't help the effort when he missed three starts with a knee injury, yet after May 22 the Indians owned a 20–10 record and were two games up in the standings.

The first year under Oscar Vitt was proceeding well by mid-summer. Through the end of June, the Indians were holding on to first place with a three-game lead over the Yankees, and Trosky was hitting the ball as well as ever. Yankees manager Joe McCarthy added some spice to the Cleveland-New York rivalry, though, when he chose one of his relief pitchers over Trosky to replace an injured Hank Greenberg on the American League All-Star team.

League president Will Harridge recommended that McCarthy pick Trosky when Greenberg dropped out, but McCarthy opted for Johnny Murphy, ostensibly on the grounds that "nobody had voted for Trosky."[23] Vitt responded the best way he knew: He had probable All-Star Game starter Bob Feller pitch a complete

Trosky crosses the plate after his sixth-inning homer against Bobo Newsom and the St. Louis Browns in the 1938 season opener. The game was played at Cleveland's Municipal Stadium, so the homer was not a "cheapie." Despite Trosky's blast, though, the Indians lost 6–2. It was an inauspicious start of Oscar Vitt's managing tenure (*Cleveland Press* Collection, Michael Schwartz Library, Cleveland State University).

game, albeit a loss, against Detroit on July 4, making it impossible for McCarthy to start the ace two days later. Part of the problem was that fan favorite Lou Gehrig was not hitting as well as Trosky, so that even though a first-baseman-for-first-baseman substitution made sense, McCarthy chose to stick it to the Indians. Upon learning that the American League had fallen to the National, 4–1, Trosky was quoted: "It served them right."

Trosky had gone home to Norway to visit his mother over the break, but 1938 still represented his best chance to crack into the All-Star "club" in the 1930s. "My teammates and even the members of the Detroit and Boston clubs think I should have at least been named to the squad. I wouldn't have cared so much if only I could have sat on the bench during the game."[24] To add insult to injury, or perhaps vice-versa, the Yankees blew past the Indians in the standings en route to another World Series title.

Son "Hal Junior," Hal and Lorraine Trosky heading home in late 1937 for the winter (*Cleveland Press* Collection, Michael Schwartz Library, Cleveland State University).

Offensively, Trosky closed the season with only 19 home runs—not even the "25 or so" he'd predicted—but drove in 110 runs and finished sixth in the batting race with an average of .334. He was also, as a by-product of hitting the ball more to left field, third in the league in doubles with 40. He finished 13th in MVP balloting that year, naturally trailing Foxx, Greenberg and DiMaggio, and for the first time placed ahead of the "Iron Horse." Gehrig had started slowly and then suffered through an uncharacteristic late-season slump. For the first time since 1925, he finished a season with a batting average below .300. It was a clear, but understandably overlooked, signal that the greatest first baseman of all time was nearing the end of his career. No one could legitimately expect the precipitous drop his performance would suffer in the first month of 1939, and certainly not that he had less than three years to live.

Hal, Lorraine and Hal Junior returned, as always, to Iowa for the long winter. It was already time to begin preparing for next season.

1939

Ah, baseball. The reason poets love the game may be that it is so often absolutely irrational. Trosky and Oscar Vitt had worked diligently the preceding year to reshape the hitter's swing, and the results had pleased player, coach, and press. Imagine, then, the player's surprise when he received his contract in the mail over the winter with no raise in salary. Trosky, arguably, had played an All-Star-worthy season in 1938, had demonstrably improved his defense, and generally played at an elite level. "We didn't give Trosky a raise," said Alva Bradley, "but he is getting really big money. He had a fairly good year in 1938, but we feel that he was well paid for it and we don't feel that he did anything to merit an increase."[25] In other words, despite the batting average and the RBI and the MVP balloting, the reduction in home runs—due to the reshaped swing and modified mental approach—justified salary stagnation. Such was baseball life in the time before free agency.

The Indians gathered in New Orleans on March 6 to renew their spring rituals, but Trosky was late. At least he had a note from the doctor: the day before, March 5, Hal and Lorraine welcomed their second son, James (later called "Jimmy"). As soon as the family was ready,

Lorraine, Hal and Hal Junior, ca. 1940. Hal was as proud of his family as he was of playing major league baseball (*Cleveland Press* Collection, Michael Schwartz Library, Cleveland State University).

Trosky headed south to Louisiana. During that spring training, Ossie Vitt asked his first baseman to become the team captain. It was an easy decision for the Iowan. The 26-year-old Trosky was able to get along with Vitt. Certainly the young Iowan had the respect of his teammates, and he quickly agreed not only for the extra $500 stipend, although that did come in handy for feeding a new baby, but because he felt that he could serve as a buffer between some of the less confident players and their vitriolic manager. Trosky became captain of a good-hitting, good-pitching team with only one major obstacle between it and a championship: the New York Yankees.

On May 1, Lou Gehrig retired after a severe decline in performance, but Joe DiMaggio and company were simply too good to let even that circumstance slow the Bombers. Instead of giving up, the Yanks never looked back and won 106 times in the regular season.

Ted Williams also made his first splash across national headlines that season, quickly joining the ranks of the greatest sluggers in the league. Until 1939, only five men had ever hit a ball into the bleachers beyond the 420-foot-mark in center field at Fenway Park: Babe Ruth, Lou Gehrig, Bill Dickey, Charlie Gehringer, and Hal Trosky. Four of those five were big and burly types, which made the gangly kid from California seem even more out of place when he smacked a ball out there early in the season. Williams would drive in 145 runs (three more than Trosky in his rookie season) and slug 31 home runs that year, many at the expense of the Tribe.

Over the first two months of the season, Trosky batted an impressive .342 and essentially continued to play the high-caliber of baseball that had characterized the previous year. He had finally integrated his natural "pull" tendencies at League Park with an "opposite field" approach for road games, and appeared to be on pace for his finest season yet. Then, on May 27 against the White Sox, Trosky stood on third when Odell Hale hit a grounder to the pitcher. Catcher Mike Tresh had the ball waiting for Trosky, as he'd been running on contact, so Trosky tried physics. Applying the unofficial baseball law of gross tonnage, he ran directly into Tresh in an effort to get the catcher to drop the ball. Tresh not only held on to the ball and recorded the out, but Trosky damaged his left shoulder to the point that he couldn't continue in the game. He wouldn't return for more than a week, finally re-entering the lineup on June 6.

The one positive of Trosky's injury was that his absence gave the team the chance to look at Oscar Grimes as a backup. Since 1934, the team had had no viable substitute for the star, but Grimes' play during Trosky's absence was sufficiently solid that both Vitt and Slapnicka agreed that the team finally had an understudy for Trosky. Trosky's return may have been too little, too late. By late June his batting average was still above .300, but all Vitt could see was the widening chasm between his team and the Yankees. He yelled and shouted for greater effort. He made snide comments to reporters about a decided under-abundance of talent in Cleveland colors. He tried to motivate by fear.

For a brief while, the tactic seemed to work. Despite saying farewell to the great Averill on June 14, trading him to Detroit for pitcher Harry Eisenstat, the Indians appeared able to win just often enough to keep Vitt from surrendering. On June 25, Ben Chapman, Trosky, and Jeff Heath hit back-to-back-to-back home runs off of Philadelphia's Lee Ross. The next man up, Ken Keltner, just barely missed making it four in a row when his fly bounced off the top of the outfield wall for a ground-rule double. Two days later, the first night game was played at the Stadium in front of 55,305 fans, and the Tribe beat the Tigers, 5–0, on a Bob Feller one-hitter. Trosky went 0-for-3 after suffering a headache all day before the game, but was still credited with an RBI, and afterward he shrugged off the headache as inconsequential.

Yet, still, Vitt screamed even louder.

At the end of July, Trosky did the unthinkable: he lifted himself from the lineup and let Grimes play a few more games at first. The official reason listed was an injured foot, but it was due to a series of severe headaches. Trosky never admitted it to the team, but there were times when his head would just throb. It was as if a fire hose had been turned on inside his skull and the water had nowhere to go; all that pressure seemed to congeal between his temples.[26] Yes, the leg certainly hurt, but it wasn't enough to keep him off the field by itself. The headaches were the tipping point and made the decision to rest an easy one.

Vitt may have assumed Trosky was just trying to motivate his teammates. Regardless, the manager did not roast Trosky in the press and did not poke fun at him behind his back. Grimes played first base well enough but, with Trosky out of the lineup, opposing pitchers didn't have to be quite as careful working to the heart of the order. A collision with Joe DiMaggio in September led to a few more days off, and the season played out in another third-place finish.

Despite his absence from the field, Ed Barrow revealed late that year that he was interested in acquiring either Trosky or Greenberg for the Yankees.[27] Trosky would likely have thrived in pinstripes, since

Yankee Stadium had the same basic right-field configuration as League Park, but neither the Indians nor the Tigers were willing to part with their sluggers, especially to an American League rival. The big men stayed put.

Such a move would likely have met with some resistance from Cleveland's fans. Ed McAuley wrote that "With the possible exception of the ever-exceptional Bob Feller, Trosky today is the most applauded of the Tribesmen."[28] Yet 1939 ended with Trosky logging only 448 at-bats for the year, and it was the first season since his 1933 overture that he appeared in fewer than 150 games. He still hit over .300 (.335) and drove in 104 runs, but it was becoming increasingly difficult to bring the necessary focus to the park each day. Hal Trosky was only 26 years old when the season ended, but the pain from a couple of notable headaches had aged him beyond his years.

Of note, in July he filed for a permanent and legal name change. While he had signed all of his contracts "Trosky," his legal name had remained "Trojovsky." That summer Judge Nelson Brewer issued an order formally changing the name to "Trosky."[29]

The Indians won 87 games that year, but still finished a whopping 19 games behind New York. Vitt promised the world that 1940 would be better. For Trosky, the end of the season was a relief, and he yearned to get home, do some farming, and find a little relief from the harsh crucible of the Cleveland press. Over the winter, almost as if according to script, the headaches faded. Trosky consulted several doctors, both in Cleveland and in Cedar Rapids, but none was able to determine the source of his agony. "They'll go away eventually," the doctors agreed when pressed for a prognosis. As the frequency of attacks decreased, the ailing slugger began to believe the doctors and threw himself into his farming, livestock, hunting and family life with new energy. By the end of the off-season, he was alive with anticipation over returning to baseball. Vitt was a complication in his life, with both positive and negative aspects, but baseball was still Trosky's game. He was even voted the "Most Popular Indian" that year in a newspaper poll of the fans, winning out over Feller and Harder. It was a baseball memory, he admitted shortly before his death, that he had cherished his whole life.[30] As it turned out, despite the physical setbacks, 1939 had been a very good year.

◈7◈

Disaster

As spring unfolded in 1940, Oscar Vitt was easing into mid-season form in the Indians' new training site in Fort Myers, Florida. As he peppered his players with insults, invective, and threats, independent observers might have concluded that the Indians were in for an interesting season. Those events, otherwise buried in the optimism of spring training, provided unmistakable indications of how the Indians would perform on the field, but not even the closest observers could have predicted the off-field drama that was gradually unfolding.

Two players, Johnny Allen and catcher Frankie Pytlak, were contractual holdouts throughout the spring. Young infielder Lou Boudreau tore cartilage in his ankle during an intra-squad game. Paul O'Dea, a promising rookie, was struck in the eye by a batting practice foul ball and never played again. Despite the adversity, though, Vitt remained outwardly buoyant.

Trosky's spring included a trip to Tampa, Florida, to play in an All-Star game. The game was a charity exhibition with the proceeds going to the Finnish Relief Fund. The fund, established and administered by former U.S. President Herbert Hoover (himself a tremendous baseball fan), channeled money to Finns displaced and hungry following the invasion by the Soviet Union the previous November. With 13,329 fans filling the stands, the game generated over $20,000 for the cause,[1] which at the time was the largest crowd ever to attend a baseball game in Florida. Jimmie Foxx, Hank Greenberg and Trosky were the American League first basemen, and the roster included the best players in the game. Joe Gordon, Bill Dickey, Ted Williams and Bob Feller were also on the squad, but despite the talent the National League still prevailed, 2–1. Still, it was something of an All-Star experience for Trosky, and he enjoyed it mightily despite going 0-for-1 at the plate as a late-inning replacement.

The Indians were optimistic as it headed north to begin the year, and when Feller opened the campaign with his famous no-hitter against the Tigers, still the only Opening Day no–hitter in Major League history, the fever spread. Trosky's season, however, started much more slowly. By the end of April Trosky was batting only .262, but the team closed out the first month with an 8–3 record. Vitt was used to success in Newark and was clearly frustrated that the Indians hadn't finished better than third in his first two seasons. The fast start by the team convinced the manager that his methods were fostering a winning environment, so he began to ramp up the pressure on his team the only way he knew: fear.

Then a near-tragedy struck the Trosky household and restored a sense of priority to Trosky. The family was now living in a larger Shaker Heights home at 1627 Kenyon, just around the corner from their previous home on Riedham Road. Lorraine was feeding her two boys at about 7:30 in the morning on May 1. She later told the reporters that, "[Fourteen-month old] Jimmie had had his cereal, orange juice, and milk and I was just feeding him a piece of crisp bacon which he seemed to swallow the wrong way because it seemed like he had just been laughing."[2] Fourteen-month-old James Trosky had actually inhaled the piece of bacon, and Lorraine rushed him to the hospital. As soon as word reached the team, Hal dropped everything and caught a cab to the airport to catch the next flight, a red-eye, to Cleveland. Trosky was a baseball player by trade, but a family man for life.

After a few days and a successful surgery at Babies and Children's Hospital in Cleveland, Jim Trosky's condition improved. When the doctors were confident that pneumonia would not set in, Hal made plans to rejoin the Indians in Washington for a series with the Senators. Frighteningly, the baby's condition abruptly took a turn for the worse, and Hal cabled Vitt that he'd be staying home until the boy got better. The Indians played, and lost, only one game during Trosky's absence, and his return naturally brought even greater optimism to the team.

The first serious fireworks of the season exploded on April 28 on the road against the Tigers. Throughout a sunny Sunday afternoon tilt against "Schoolboy" Rowe, and in front of a crowd of over 30,000, the Tribe lineup ran through the Detroit staff like the proverbial hot knife through butter. The Indians entered the ninth inning of that game with a 9–3 lead and victory assured. Cleveland starter Al Milnar, along with the Indians relievers, figuratively self-destructed and the Tigers tied the score at nine runs apiece while batting around. At this point, Oscar Vitt was reportedly "mugging" on the bench and criticizing everyone in sight. Trosky homered with two out in the tenth inning to win the game, but Vitt was not mollified.

The next day Feller was off his game and lost to the Tigers, 4–3. Vitt stooped to visibly criticizing his superhuman pitcher. No one was safe, and the feeling was that each player was only as good, or bad, as his last play. According to the wisdom of the ages, or at least the baseball sages, the game is one that can only be played well in a state of relaxed tension. That sounds like psychological doubletalk or coachspeak at first blush, but it makes sense for the tasks inherent to the game. Unlike most sports such as football or hockey, where sheer effort and adrenaline can elevate a person's performance, hitting a baseball is even more difficult if the batter is rigid with tension. The same applies to throwing and catching. Relaxation is vital to the game, and the Indians' manager was pushing them in the completely opposite direction.

Vitt's team was quickly approaching meltdown. It didn't help Vitt's disposition that Trosky had homered twice on April 30 before flying to his son's bedside, and then replacement Oscar Grimes took a batting practice line drive to the face on May 3 and suffered a fractured left cheek. Grimes' surgery took more than two hours, and the team had no idea when he might return.[3] Vitt was left with a hole in the center of his lineup.

A week later, the team beat the Yankees twice to begin an improbable climb toward first place. Hal Trosky was warming up as well. On May 7, he hammered his fifth and final career home run off Lefty Grove at Fenway Park. Grove was just over a year from retirement, wrapping up a career in which he won exactly 300 games in 17 years with a lifetime ERA of just 3.06. The pride of coal country in Lonaconing, Maryland, he'd worked in a glass factory, among other places, as a young man and only began throwing a baseball when he turned 17. He was such a sensation that the minor league Martinsburg Mountaineers quickly sold him to Jack Dunn and the Baltimore Orioles, where he won over 25 games three times in five years.

Dunn sold Grove to his old friend Connie Mack in late 1924, and by 1927 he was a 20-game winner. He had reached that mark seven times by 1936, but in 1940 he still had the fire that had carried him through the years. Trosky's eighth-inning shot that May afternoon put him in another elite circle. Only five players hit five or more homers off of Grove. That list included Charlie Gehringer, Hank Greenberg, Babe Ruth, and Lou Gehrig; Hal Trosky became the fifth.

Through Memorial Day, Trosky had 11 homers and the Indians were locked into second place with a 23–13 mark. But Vitt's methods were wearing thin on his charges. "I'd walk out on the field before the game," *Plain-Dealer* reporter Gene Whitney recalled in 1960, 20 years after the fact, "and he'd [Vitt] call me over. Right off he'd run down the lineup, blistering everybody. It became monotonous and tedious and after a while none of us paid any attention to it."[4]

On the surface, this was an Indians team that appeared ready to challenge for the American League pennant, but the daily performance was never good enough for their acerbic manager. Oscar Vitt was not a failed human being, but he was on dangerous ground as a baseball manager. Within the Cleveland leadership circle, there was no system of checks and balances that could temper his actions, either. As alluded to earlier, the term "Indians organization" was a bit oxymoronic. There was Alva Bradley, there was the legal team, there was Slapnicka in his ill-defined and non-specific role, and there was Vitt. By some accounts, the latter two did not get along well. Vitt was fixated on winning ball games, tone deaf to the words he was using in handling his players and in discussing them with the media, and all the while with Slapnicka more than willing to make a change if he found the manager wanting. Additionally, Slapnicka's relationship with Trosky and Feller, as fellow Iowans, gave their opinions greater credibility than Vitt's, which widened the chasm between team an manager even more. In retrospect, it would have been shocking if the powder keg hadn't ignited.

Even when confronted with stories such as Jeff Heath and another player staging a fight in the hope that Vitt would attempt to break it up so Heath could "accidently" take a shot at the manager, "Ole Os" refused to take the bait and engage his team directly, instead preferring to communicate via the press. "I guess it can't be helped," Vitt told reporters. "I'll just go along doing the best I can and the boys will have to like it."[5] Those words, corroborated by other quotations attributed to Vitt, are consistent with the notion that "Doctor Os" showed one face (and tongue) to the press, while saving his more caustic "Mr. Vitt" for his team. The players felt their manager was antagonistic and spiteful, but the press at the time portrayed him as suffering and misunderstood. It was a bizarre, "Jekyll-and-Hyde" situation.

Yet, since the Indians' manager remained a vision of confidence to those reporters, there was little to package for public consumption. Vitt told the press that Cleveland just might unseat the Yankees. To a collection of writers who had spent the previous four years chronicling the Bronx wrecking ball as it won pennant after pennant by at least 11 games each season, this was likely more akin to hysterical babble than to a serious assessment of the balance of power. To the players, it was business as usual. Vitt had, according to Robert Creamer in his book *Baseball in '41*, an "abrasive, sarcastic tongue and he used it freely."[6] He had a pet criticism for each of his players, even calling young Bill Zuber "scatter arm." Zuber later said that "playing under Vitt was the worst experience I've ever had."[7]

Some of his big league lessons were valuable, such as convincing Trosky to hit to the left side and showing Bob Feller how to better hold runners by slightly lowering his high leg kick. As capable a technician as he was, Oscar Vitt was not ideally suited for the role of major league manager.

Vitt, as did many in the day, managed his first two seasons in Cleveland from the coaching box instead of assuming a more detached post in the dugout. In retrospect, though, the manager's greatest flaw may have been that he never truly learned to lead. He certainly understood the game, but evinced little concept of how to rally and unite his players. Evidence that motivation by fear often fails since, at some point, the "motivated" may decide they have less to lose in rebellion than they do in maintaining the status quo, fills the shelves of leadership literature, but Vitt was old-school (even for the time). One young Cleveland pitcher, Ken Jungels, was later quoted in *Oldtyme Baseball News*: "I was a young player sitting on the bench, and I could not believe my ears. Here was a Major League manager calling players names with religious and ethnic hatreds. It was very upsetting."[8] Certainly, as author L. P. Hartley observed, the past is indeed a foreign country, and they did things differently there, but even for people who lived in that age, Vitt's behavior was still beyond normal boundaries.

Cleveland pitching then figuratively, the Tribe split a doubleheader with the lowly Senators, only narrowly avoiding the sweep. Vitt was furious with Al Milnar for his performance, despite the win, and said as much to the press. Some players even claimed to overhear Vitt yearning for his Newark Bears team, with the none-too-subtle implication that those minor leaguers were a better group than the current Indians squad. Opinion did not change at all when, on June 7, the Indians lost to the Yankees—despite Trosky's 14th four-bagger—on (among other indignities) George Selkirk's steal of home off Bob Feller.

On June 10, the Indians were rained out in Boston and the players spent the day in the hotel lobby, dissecting their misfortune. The blame, naturally, fell on Vitt. Some of the players advanced the idea of mutiny, of trying to dump the manager, but team captain Trosky counseled patience. The slugger was a proud baseball veteran and wanted no part of public finger-pointing, even though he had been repeatedly stung by Vitt's acerbic "coaching." A few days earlier, Trosky had asked Vitt if he could skip batting practice since it was raining that afternoon and the big man was recovering from a nasty cold. "Why don't you," Vitt chided, "you're not doing us any good."[9]

The next day the Red Sox blew out the Indians. Vitt was in rare form during the game, again screaming about his star: "Look at him [Feller]! He's supposed to be my ace. I'm supposed to win a pennant with that kind of pitching?"[10] This time, according to some of the papers, Vitt yelled a bit too loud, and Feller heard him all the way out on the mound. For any athlete, especially a young one like Feller, genuine confidence is rarely a long suit. Feller had all of the necessary tools of the trade, but was still just a 22-year-old whose daily performance brought the scrutiny of the national sporting press. Every victory was "huge," every shortfall "disastrous." Feller was also, quietly, playing hurt.

That evening, Trosky spoke with Frank Gibbons of the *Cleveland Press*. He told the reporter that the Indians could win the pennant with their current players, but had no chance as long as Vitt was the manager. Gibbons cautioned Trosky to wait and see how things turned out before doing anything rash. It was the same advice Trosky had just given his teammates.

The player didn't mention his own problems. He did not tell Gibbons that his headaches were stronger and were lasting longer than the year before.[11] And he didn't tell anyone that consistently hitting a pitched baseball while feeling like he had a railroad spike driven between his ears was nearly impossible. His pride would not possibly permit such disclosure, and he knew just how difficult it would be to engender even the slightest public sympathy for a man making more than $10,000 just to play baseball six months out of a year.

In the hotel lobby the next morning, the players checked out early. At breakfast, they continued surreptitiously plotting how to solve the Vitt problem. During the game that afternoon, which the Indians lost, Vitt snidely sniped at Mel Harder. "It's about time you won one, the money you're getting." To the players, this was rock bottom. Mel Harder had been with the team for 11 years and was thoroughly respected by every member of the organization.

Except one.

Harder could only respond, "I gave you the best I had."

On the train ride from Boston to Cleveland, no one bothered to break out the cards. Ben Chapman and Rollie Hemsley reportedly called Boudreau and Ray Mack into their berth and told the young infielders that some of the players were circulating a petition calling for Vitt's ouster. The two young infielders, along with Al Smith, Beau Bell, Mike Naymick and Soup Campbell, were excused from participating.

"You're too young in baseball," Ben Chapman told them, "and if any of this should backfire it could ruin your careers." It was a gesture that demonstrated the deadly seriousness of the mutineers. Mel Harder and Johnny Allen, in a meeting with the rest of the players, told the team that they would go to owner Alva Bradley alone. The rest of the team disagreed, arguing that they should all confront the owner together in a unified front, but they did appoint Harder as their voice.

On June 13, the same day that the Nazis overran Paris, more tragedy struck Trosky. Just as the train pulled into the Cleveland Station, Trosky received word that his mother had died suddenly and unexpectedly in Iowa. Trosky went straight from the train station to the airport, while Harder called Alva Bradley's office, seeking an appointment with the owner. Instead of sending Harder alone, ten of the dissidents went to Bradley's office en masse to show the executive how deep their grievances went.

The players were all seasoned veterans who knew how baseball was played, both as a game and as a business. They were also men who played in times before the advent of the "spoiled superstars," men who worked in the off-season not by choice but out of necessity, and they were men who understood the consequences of their actions. Clearly, this was no idle grumbling about a stern taskmaster. Vitt had wounded them deeply enough to spur them to extraordinary measures.

The players told Bradley that Vitt had to go if the team was to compete successfully. They outlined four specific grievances, each of which Bradley later confirmed, and demanded the owner take action. Trosky even telephoned Bradley from the airport to ensure his absence wouldn't be misconstrued as disagreement. Despite his personal misgivings about the action, the team captain would not stand idly by while his teammates pressed the issue.

Bradley told the players that he would look into the matter and warned them that if word of the meeting were released, the players would he ridiculed forever. Naturally, someone leaked the story to Gordon Cobbledick almost immediately. While the Indians won the game that afternoon, the insurrection was front page news the following morning. The headline for the story was, physically, larger on the printed page than that afforded to Hitler's invasion of Paris. Even Trosky's hometown paper, the *Cedar Rapids Gazette*, jumped on the bandwagon and bashed the "Crybaby Indians" as vehemently as newspaper space and Midwestern restraint would permit.

Aftermath

Gordon Cobbledick tackled the issue head-on. "Is Oscar Vitt a good manager? The answer, in light of yesterday's developments, apparently is NO! For the first requisite for a good manager is that he convinces his players of his qualifications for the job. And Vitt failed in that!"

The exclamation marks underscore the emotion and astonishment surrounding the players' actions. "Cobbie" continued with what remains one of the fairest assessments of the relationship:

> A good manager is one who gets the most of his ballplayers. He may finish last, but if he has kept his men playing to their ability, small though it may be, he is a better manager than a rival who barely sneaks into first place with a team of Ruths, Gehrigs.... No one has ever accused Vitt of ignorance of baseball tactics and strategy. But baseball tactics and strategy are pretty well standardized. In most situations there is only one "right" thing to do. In others, there are seldom more than two and the good manager is the fellow who makes the better guess. But a major league manager's success depends about 10 percent on his tactical

soundness and 90 percent on his ability to handle men. The Indians say it is difficult to hustle for Vitt. They charge that he has destroyed their spirit and wrecked the incentive to play winning hall. It isn't merely that they dislike him, for other managers have been disliked by their players and still made a success. Their chief complaint is that he has forfeited their respect and caused them to lose face with other teams.[12]

One Iowa writer contacted Trosky at home, where he was still grieving for his mother, and asked the player about the mini-drama in Cleveland. Trosky answered,

> Those writers know the situation so well that I couldn't add anything to what they have already stated. The boys are sincere in their complaints. Take Bob Feller for example. Bob is the kind who never did anybody any harm. But he was among the leaders in the ouster movement. He must feel justified. It's the same with the rest.... There's a lot of defense offered for Vitt, namely, that he must have a lot of ability because he is keeping his team near the top of the league. But that is misleading. We are up there because the Yankees have not yet come into their own. But we're only playing only .575 ball. That isn't championship stuff. Our showing is due mainly to the failures of some other teams.[13]

Trosky spoke about Bob Feller again. "Due to Vitt [Feller has had] a lot more bad days already than he should have had." That would plague the Indians to the end. Not even Bob Feller had a mechanical arm—though some hitters would probably swear otherwise—and Vitt simply overworked his star. Bradley went on the record, saying that he would take no immediate action regarding his manager or his players until he had a chance to talk with the team captain.[14]

Later in his life, while not formally discussing the incident, Trosky shared his memories with *Des Moines Register* writer Maury White. After one particularly frustrating episode in 1939, a game during which Vitt infuriated the team by giving the "choke" sign to one of his own players, Trosky said, "We had a meeting and some wanted to confront Vitt then. I talked them out of it." By 1940, there were more frequent anti–Vitt meetings. Trosky further observed that "I never attended a single one of those meetings. I wasn't even at the one on the train when they set the rebellion. When the train got to Cleveland, I got word that my mother had died and caught a plane immediately for home."[15]

The Indians called Trosky in Iowa and asked him to return to the team as soon as possible. It was the day of his mother's funeral. "When I got back [after the funeral] and walked on to the field, I was booed. I was an ass in Cleveland forever after. They laid it on me. And I hadn't led the revolt in any way."[16] The fans punished Trosky more than the other Indians at a time when sympathy should surely have been with him. "When we were going to have the showdown, Trosky wasn't the leader, but he was one of them.... [It] was more of a group effort."[17] Franklin Lewis was perhaps the writer most guilty of trying to pin the blame tail on the Trosky donkey. In his 1949 book on the Indians, he all but accused Trosky of being the godfather of the revolt, even though every account of those involved at the time agreed that there was no single spearhead. Of course, players didn't have social media with which to make their case to the public. They relied on the press to offer some sort of balance. But this was sports, and nothing more. Partisanship encouraged readership, which in turn generated advertising revenue and subscriptions. Lewis' version has been largely debunked over time, but the reality that his version was the first told gave it more gravity than it deserved. Trosky forgave the fans, even understood their angst, but the psychic wounds inflicted by the various scribes never healed. His son, Hal Junior, often observed that "The Vitt affair affected his heart. He was a man of honor, he was a man of responsibility, and he was a man of empathy. What happened with Vitt bothered him for the rest of his life."[18]

Even more damning to the "suits," however, was a memo from Alva Bradley which was only discovered (and published) by the *Cleveland News* in 1951:

> We should have won the pennant.... Our real trouble started when a group of 10 players came to my office and made four distinct charges against [Vitt] and asked for his dismissal. The four charges made against Vitt, on investigations I have made, were 100% correct.[19]

Bradley offered the job to popular coach Luke Sewell, but the latter demurred. Sewell, brother of Indians Hall of Famer Joe, later said:

> Oscar was a fine fellow, but he talked too much. He would say things, promise things, which he forgot he ever said or promised. Players resented this because they thought he did it on purpose. But he didn't.... [The rebellion] was not all Oscar's fault. The [players] were to blame, too. They picked on one another, blamed each other when things went wrong, and blew a pennant they should have won.[20]

The owner did not wish to fire Vitt outright but preferred to ease him out under the guise of poor health, introduce Sewell as interim manager, and then make the arrangement permanent after the season.

Sewell wanted the managerial job and would likely have accepted the offer had the team fired Vitt in 1940, but he wanted absolutely no part of any sort of mealy-mouthed executive ambivalence.

On June 17, the day after the players were chastised by the fans while sweeping a doubleheader from Philadelphia, the *Plain-Dealer* printed a statement drafted by Alva Bradley and signed by 21 players: "We the undersigned publicly declare to withdraw all statements referring to the resignation of Oscar Vitt. We feel this action is for the betterment of the Cleveland Baseball Club."[21]

Roy Weatherly refused to sign it and walked out of the meeting even before the signing was over. Jeff Heath and Hank Helf also did not sign (they were both in the hospital and thus not present for the meeting), and Oscar Grimes' signature is missing only because he was still recovering from his head wound. Otherwise, the team made a public effort to move on. Even Vitt, a man who might justifiably have felt wounded, tried to shrug off the protest. The June 20 *Sporting News* ran a cover photo of Vitt and Alva Bradley sitting in an office, smiles on both faces, as the two "discussed" the players' demand for his resignation. Vitt put up the appearance of not riding his players too hard. But Vitt's tenure with the Indians was doomed. It would have been easy for him to sabotage the team with some innocuous moves later in the season: Pulling an effective pitcher early, leaving a tired one in for an extra inning, unusual infield adjustments, and the like. That would hit the players in the wallet in terms of lost post-season money. But the manager may have realized that if he lost, he'd be blamed, and if he somehow won, Bradley would still likely fire him and he'd he seeking work with another team.

Still, it was a dumpster fire. It stunk, and nothing good was going to come of the whole affair. Gordon Cobbledick observed that the Indians had become "the most unpopular team" in major league baseball, and Vitt must certainly have been the most scrutinized manager.[22]

Independence Day in Detroit was a low-water mark for the "Crybabies." Almost 58,000 fans jammed Briggs Stadium for the duel between the league leaders. Mostly, though, they seemed bent on taunting the Tribe. The fans hung diapers along the stands, a la traditional post-season bunting, wore baby clothes and huge infant bottles for hats, and even threw toy baby balls onto the field. They cheered Vitt even as the teams split the twin bill.

Here Is Facsimile of Indians' Peace Pact

THE CLEVELAND BALL COMPANY
LEAGUE PARK
CLEVELAND, OHIO

We the undersigned publicly declare to withdraw all statements referring to the resignation of Oscar Vitt. We feel this action is for the betterment of the Cleveland Baseball Club.

Above are the signatures of the 21 Cleveland Indians and the statement which was drafted in the clubhouse following yesterday's game. 6-17-1940

A facsimile of the Indians players' signed statement to the fans regarding the reported insurrection against manager Oscar Vitt. The apology did not have the intended effect, though, as the team was pilloried for the rest of the season in every city they visited, and they have been labeled the "Crybaby Indians" ever since (*Cleveland Plain Dealer*, June 17, 1940).

7. *Disaster*

Trosky and Vitt had a brief on-the-field tiff over strategy during the first game. The Indians trailed Detroit and Vitt wanted to bring in Johnny Allen in relief. Trosky and several others argued with Vitt, imploring the manager to save Allen for the second game, and Vitt relented. In the second game, a fresh Allen pitched well and helped seal the Indians' victory. A week later, Vitt renamed Trosky team captain—the last player so designated until Vic Wertz was tabbed fifteen years later—perhaps as a gesture of truce, or simply a necessary step in calming the waters, and the on-field performance improved.

Perhaps the catharsis of finally clearing the air was effective. The Indians played their best ball of the year, at least for a time, but the magic faded. By mid–July, the American League race was a seesaw. The Indians were in first place at the All-Star Game break, but dropped six games shortly after the break. Fortunately for Cleveland, the Tigers also played poorly and thus kept the drama alive.

On August 11 in St. Louis, Trosky swung his way into the history books by becoming the 17th American Leaguer to clout 200 home runs (the league commemorated the feat with a certificate that Trosky kept for the rest of his life). Several days later, he pulled a muscle in his right leg. The days off were well-timed, as the headaches were again attacking with such ferocity that he began having trouble even seeing the baseball. In the August 31 edition of the *Plain-Dealer*, Cobbledick acknowledged Trosky's vision troubles. He noted that the slugger's eyesight had gotten so bad that it "has compelled him to wear glasses off the field." Trosky's eyes were fine. It was his head that was the source of his pain.

But not the only source.

The season pushed into September, and in a game against (who else) Schoolboy Rowe and the Tigers, Trosky bent over to rub some dirt on his hands before batting. As he did so, he accidentally picked up some tiny shards of glass and sliced his right thumb. The next time at bat he wore a batting glove with no thumb. Birdie Tebbetts, the Tigers' catcher, noticed the glove but didn't say anything, as teammate Hank Greenberg had used just such a glove earlier in the year after a similar injury.

Trosky, this time, stepped into Rowe's 0–2 mistake and launched it into the right-centerfield gap for an inside-the-park home run. The next time Trosky came up to bat, Tebbetts spoke up and reminded the umpire that the glove was actually illegal. Trosky was furious. After grudgingly removing the offending glove and replacing it with tape, Trosky blistered Rowe's next offering into right field.

"Hah!" yelled Tebbetts down to the big slugger as he stood on first. "Held you to a single!"

Trosky fouled out to first during his next plate appearance, and gave way to pinch-hitter Oscar Grimes in the seventh. On the day Trosky went 2–3 with two runs scored and an RBI, it was likely a satisfying afternoon for the big first baseman.

The teams continued to jockey with other down the stretch of an unusual event: an American League pennant race not involving the Yankees. After four years of total New York domination, the Tigers entered the last weekend of the season in Cleveland needing only one win to clinch the flag.

More than 45,000 semi-rabid fanatics made their way into Cleveland Stadium that weekend to cheer Feller in his quest for victory number one (of the three required) to reach the World Series. One local radio station had whipped up a revenge-on-Detroit frenzy, and many of those attending the game were armed with overripe fruit and vegetables—perfect missiles for heaving at the enemy Tigers.

Fans and press alike debated whether Feller would face the hated Rowe, curveballer extraordinaire Tommy Bridges, or even Bobo Newsom. The answer was none of them. Just before the teams took the field, Floyd Giebell, a career loser in both the major and minor leagues, was announced as the Tigers' starter.

As it turned out, manager Del Baker was brilliant. He knew the Tigers had to win but one of the three to clinch the pennant. He also knew that Feller could, on any given day, approach perfection. Even a great effort by one of his merely mortal hurlers could be obviated by a couple of hours of Feller-ian magnificence. Baker couldn't guarantee that his team would muster even a single hit, much less a run. Why not, he decided, sacrifice this game and go after the last two? Giebell had appeared in exactly one game since being recalled from the minor leagues ten days earlier, and had only posted a 15–16 record for the year in the lower levels. Feller, on the other hand, had been little less than dominant, posting a 22–10 record, and would eventually lead the American League in wins, shutouts (4), complete games (31), innings pitched (320.1) and strikeouts (261).

7. Disaster

Feller against Giebell. David against Goliath. Game on.

Feller proved as good as his reputation in holding the Tigers to a mere three hits. Unfortunately, one of those blows was Rudy York's 2-run homer in the fourth inning. With Cleveland stymied by the 30-year-old Giebell, and unable to convert any of their six hits into runs, the Tigers won 2–0.

Down south, in Cincinnati, Bill McKechnie's Reds were completing their own remarkable 100-win season, winning the pennant by 12 games over the Dodgers. Had Cleveland prevailed, the World Series would have been an all-Ohio affair. It was not to be.

Vitt's situation also played out according to expectation. The manager said goodbye to each of the players after the finale and wished them all well but, as Eugene Whitney reported, "A few (of the players) left the dressing room without a word of farewell."[23] On October 8, as Detroit was losing to Cincinnati in a seven-game World Series, Bradley drew the curtain and fired Oscar Vitt. He replaced the manager with Roger Peckinpaugh, who had himself been replaced at the Tribe's helm by Walter Johnson back in 1933.

Vitt's three-season record as manager was 262–198, and yielded one second- and two third-place finishes. He did as well as anyone could have, outside New York, in 1938 and 1939. But what of 1940? Could the Indians have won the pennant without Vitt driving the players to

Hal and Lorraine Trosky, circa late 1940. The couple met while growing up in Norway, Iowa, and married before the 1934 season. Their marriage lasted some 45 years and produced four children, including major leaguer Hal Junior (*Cleveland Press* Collection, Michael Schwartz Library, Cleveland State University).

mutiny and without the ensuing media attention surrounding the "Crybaby" incident? Maybe Vitt was too distracting. Maybe his harsh methods spurred the Indians to extraordinary levels of production. The subject is moot.

Trosky finished the season batting only .295, and his 93 RBI marked his first full major league season without at least 100 runs. The headaches had hit hard in August and September, but he loathed missing any game in the tight pennant race. He still crushed 39 doubles and led the team with 25 home runs, but the leg injury and family tragedies left the team short at the end.

The "Crybaby" affair has marred the perception of that team's legacy for generations, but the larger view shows the incident as just a sub-plot in a fascinating season. 1940, as exciting as it was for baseball writ large, was only an appetizer for the great 1941 season to come. For Trosky, though, 1941 would prove to be the beginning of the end.

As a postscript to the whole affair, one year later the following appeared in the September 28, 1941, *Cleveland Plain Dealer*:

> Oscar Vitt disclosed today he had resigned as manager of the manager of the Portland baseball club which finished last in the Coast League this season. The former Cleveland Indians' manager submitted his resignation at the close of the season.... Vitt expressed belief that if the Portland club had had a few more replacements it probably could have finished well up in the first division.

The following year, 1942, would be Vitt's last as a baseball manager.

❖8❖

Cleveland Sunset

"There's nothing mysterious about [strategy], is there?" That basic truth, offered to Franklin Lewis by returning manager Roger Peckinpaugh,[1] was the basis of his approach to his second term as Cleveland Indians manager. It was actually his third stint with the team. From 1910–1912, he played 81 games at shortstop for Nap Lajoie's Clevelanders. After eight seasons with the Yankees and five with Washington, he had closed out his playing career with 60 games for the White Sox. Many at the time agreed, Peckinpaugh first among them, that the man knew his baseball.

In 1928, the Indians hired "Peck" to manage the team, a task he performed fairly well. Up until Bradley fired him in 1933, he posted only one losing season (1928, when his charges posted a 62–92 mark), and his re-hiring for 1941 was welcomed by many of the players who had soured on the Vitt experiment. Alva Bradley had tried several times to coerce Luke Sewell to take the reins, but Sewell refused out of a combination of loyalty to Vitt and disgust with the players' actions in the rebellion. Sewell, in fact, moved to St. Louis shortly thereafter and began 1941 as manager of the Browns.

The Indians infield of 1941 featured Trosky at first, Ray Mack at second (a 1940 All-Star), Lou Boudreau at shortstop (another 1940 All-Star), and fielding genius Ken Keltner at third. They weren't fearsome like, say, the Detroit Tigers infield of 1934, but were still a formidable unit in their own right. "The Tribe has achieved the apparently contradictory feat of standing pat on its essential make-up ... and at the same time has made more changes in the squad than have been made in any single winter for several years."[2] The team certainly had not forgotten the events of 1940—prominently pinned to a bulletin board in the clubhouse was a *Cleveland News* clipping of a picture of

Vitt in his new, 1941 Portland Beavers uniform, captioned, "Back to the Bushes"—but were collectively eager to focus on improving on the results from last year. The Tigers, Peckinpaugh believed, were clearly beatable, while the Yankees were regrouping after their epic four-year dominance in the late 1930s and posed a lesser threat.

The arrival of Lou Boudreau was one of the highlights of the Vitt

era. The infielder had been summoned to Cleveland in 1938 after only 60 games at Class B Cedar Rapids. He had been signed as a prospective third baseman, but Ken Keltner had a legitimate lock on that position, so Boudreau moved over to shortstop. By 1939 he was through with the minors and played one-third of the season in the Cleveland infield.

Still considered one of the better defensive shortstops ever, Boudreau's lifetime .295 batting average was legitimate, and his sneaky power was evidenced in leading the league in doubles three times. In 1942 he would be named player-manager, and in his nine years at the Indians' helm he posted a 728–649 record, a stint that included Cleveland's second World Series title in 1948. That year was

Hal poses with eldest son Hal Junior in the family's backyard in 1941. Hal Trosky, Jr., was highly sought after as a high school slugging star in Cedar Rapids, but after a violent collision in the minors, he retrained himself as a pitcher. He was talented enough to throw a no-hitter in the minors, and earned a brief appearance with the Chicago White Sox in 1951. His lifetime major league pitching record was 1–0 (*Cleveland Press* Collection, Michael Schwartz Library, Cleveland State University).

Boudreau's finest as a player. In addition to managing the team, he played in 152 games while batting .355 and driving in 106 runs. Boudreau the shortstop, it turned out, was one of manager Boudreau's most effective weapons, as he was voted the American League MVP. In 1941, though, he was still just a 23-year-old infielder on a troubled team.

Trosky suffered that year, reflected by his lowest batting average since the sophomore season of 1935 while looking to climb back over the 100-RBI mark. Trosky voluntarily surrendered his captaincy, giving up the $500 stipend just to be able to start the year with a complete focus on improving his own game. Peckinpaugh not only accepted his resignation, he did not appoint a successor.

One of Trosky's spring experiments was to dust off the switch-hitting tactic, and at one point in March he told reporters that there was a 50–50 chance that he'd use it in the regular season. "I've been thinking about that plan all winter, and I have complete confidence I can accomplish it. If I do, I should add quite a few points to my batting average, for some of those smart left-handers give me plenty of trouble."[3]

The team broke camp in Florida and headed north with a better bullpen, an improved outfield, and a calmer clubhouse. The 1941 season began with none of the flourish which surrounded Feller's no-hitter the year before. Trosky's headaches continued, though, striking with no notice and leaving a wide wake of debilitating pain. One day early in the season, catcher Rollie Hemsley stumbled in on the big man using an ice pack to relieve the pain immediately before a game. When asked if the headaches were affecting his play, Trosky finally admitted the truth. He reluctantly acknowledged that it wasn't the pain that was so troublesome as much as it was the vision loss. For a man who made a living by smiting baseballs, he was powerless against a blurry, white apparition that he said sometimes looked "like a bunch of white feathers." Even Lorraine was getting scared. She knew that her husband could accidentally step into an inside pitch and suffer the same fate that had befallen Ray Chapman 21 years earlier, when he died after being hit in the head by a Carl Mays fastball.

This was an era in which pitchers owned the outside of the plate, and any hitter seeking an advantage by creeping closer to home plate was liable to end up with a ball aimed at his ear. The courage to face this threat comes in part from the batter's confidence in his ability to see and react to the ball. Without being able to see the pitch, he wasn't able to set himself into a productive hitting position and was forced to defensively stab at the ball instead of attacking it. Trosky played less and less. When he did take the field, he was effective only when the migraines subsided.

According to *The Sporting News*, "Trosky hesitates to make a definite connection between his relatively poor record this year and the pain that thumps through his cranium 'at least half the time,' but he admits that the physical trouble causes him loss of sleep and upsets his nervous system."[4] He acknowledged that he could not "go on like this forever. If I can't find some cure for these headaches, I'll have to give up and retire to my farm in Iowa."[5] It wasn't as if he hadn't tried just about every possible remedy for the pain. From dietary changes to relaxation to medicine, he tried them all, and each provided the same result. The headaches returned.

In early June, he suffered through a 2-for-32 slump, and in a single week the Indians watched a four-game lead in the standings ebb to one. The club was streaky. For every winning streak there was an associated skid. By the time the season ended, the team had posted two-plus consecutive wins 22 times. Unfortunately, this was balanced by 19 streaks of two-plus consecutive losses. The team was either hot or cold. The average of the two temperatures, like Cleveland's season, was tepid. At best.

In late June Peckinpaugh held a team meeting and told the team that it needed to fix its "mental outlook." The pep talk helped for a bit, but as with the rest of the year, the tide again turned. Trosky had returned after a few days off following a shoulder injury. While Oscar Grimes had performed well in their star slugger's absence, the team welcomed back the Bohemian. "For some reason," Ed McAuley wrote, "not satisfactorily explained by his [batting] average the last two years, Trosky is generally considered the bellwether of the Indians. His teammates look to him for leadership."[6] Unfortunately, for the 1941 Indians, the team needed more than just leadership; it needed a few more runs.

The 1941 season was the last one before the upheaval of the 1940s. By the time the smoke cleared from the attack on Pearl Harbor that December, some of the best major leaguers entered the military, leaving the game to an earnest but less talented group of substitutes. Once the war ended, Jackie Robinson and Larry Doby would change the field forever by putting a dagger into the de facto racial segregation in baseball. So 1941 was the final year of "old" baseball, and in that year Trosky and the Indians were part of one of the most lauded feats in the history of the game.

DiMaggio's Streak

Most of the world's population today was not even alive when Joe DiMaggio retired in 1951, but his 56-consecutive game hitting streak in 1941 remains one of the safest, least assailed marks in all of sport. It began, as many such achievements do, without fanfare. On May 15, the day after DiMaggio went hitless against a pitcher he often referred to as the toughest he ever faced–Mel Harder—he began with a single in a loss to the White Sox. From that point on, DiMaggio's streak grew and grew and, ultimately, captured the nation.

DiMaggio faced the Indians six times during the streak. In a June 1 doubleheader at Cleveland Stadium, he singled off Al Milnar in game one and off Mel Harder in the nightcap. Those were games 17 and 18 in the streak, and the Yankees' sweep knocked Cleveland out of first place in the American League standings.

The newspaper account described the single off Harder as pulled down the left field line after glancing off third baseman Ken Keltner's glove. The memory of that hit evidently stayed with Keltner, for when the teams met again in mid–July, he played DiMaggio much closer to the base, a move which had enormous consequences for the streak.

On June 2, the Yankees were told of Lou Gehrig's imminent death, and while the Iron Horse's condition was no secret, his passing clearly affected his former teammates. New York played a distracted game, and the crowd of 8,000 was treated to two DiMaggio hits, and a 7–5 Indians win (despite Trosky's 0-for-11 performance during the three-game series). Feller pitched well enough to win, but the first Yankees run in the second inning ended the pitcher's personal 30-consecutive-scoreless-innings streak.

On June 14, in New York, media attention had elevated as DiMaggio prepared to break the Yankees record of 29 consecutive games with a hit. Ironically, that record was set by none other than Tribe manager

Roger Peckinpaugh. Gradually at first, then explosively, the nation's attention turned to DiMaggio's streak.

In League Park on July 16, DiMaggio got three hits in front of 15,000 fans in a 10–3 Yankees win. "The Streak" had reached 56 games. The July 17 game was scheduled for Cleveland Stadium, and 67,468 passed the turnstiles at the lakefront to watch him get another in his 57th game.

Trosky was on the bench, not feeling well again, so Oscar Grimes started at first base. Al Smith took the mound for Cleveland, although Jim Bagby eventually replaced him. Joe DiMaggio smacked two rockets down the third base line, but Ken Keltner (clearly remembering DiMaggio's ability to pull the ball) was playing close to the bag and was able to backhand both. DiMaggio also smashed a ground ball at Boudreau which threatened to handcuff the shortstop, but he knocked it down and turned it into a deceptively easy double play. He also walked once.

In the ninth inning, with DiMaggio hitless but the Yankees leading, 4–1, New York manager Joe McCarthy brought in Johnny Murphy in relief of Lefty Gomez. Murphy, one of the first of the "modern relievers," was apparently not quite ready and let the first two Indians reach base before yielding a triple to pinch-hitter Larry Rosenthal to close the score to 4–3.

Trosky pinch-hit, but instead of delivering a sacrifice fly to score Rosenthal, all he could manage was a grounder to first baseman Johnny Sturm. Soup Campbell followed with a dribbler to the pitcher, and Rosenthal was eliminated in a run-down off third base. Roy Weatherly ended the game by grounding out. Had Trosky delivered the fly ball to score the tying run, DiMaggio would have had another at-bat in extra innings. That is not insignificant, considering DiMaggio began another 16-game hitting streak the next day.

End of the Line

By midsummer, the migraines were past unbearable and well into the realm of torturous. In August, Cleveland began a seven-game road trip without their bomber. Trosky stayed home, with Oscar Grimes assuming first base duties, primarily because the headaches frequently left him non-functional on the diamond. "Hal's headaches were terrible,

terrible," remembered pitcher Harry Eisenstat. "They'd sometimes hit him in the middle of the game. But he'd keep playing; he wouldn't come out."[7]

Trosky did join the team for the last stop, Chicago. In the opening game of an August 17 doubleheader at Comiskey Park, Trosky delivered two singles off White Sox ace Ted Lyons and scored one of Cleveland's two runs. In the sixth inning, Lyons led off for the Sox and hit a dribbler to third. Trosky fielded Keltner's throw but collided with the Chicago pitcher and suffered a broken thumb, fractured in two places. He left the game, and in walking off the field at Comiskey Park took his final stroll in Cleveland colors. The slugger missed the final 39 games of the season. It was impossible to know it that day, but the next time Hal Trosky would play a major league game would be almost three years later, in 1944, on that same Comiskey Park diamond, also in a White Sox-Indians game. Trosky, however, would be wearing Chicago's uniform.

The year had started with a bang, as son Lynn was born in January, but ended with a professional whimper. The Indians finished in a tie for fourth place with the Tigers, and their old first baseman drove in only 51 runs in 310 at-bats. Every first baseman in the league, with the exception of Yankee Johnny Sturm, drove in more runs than Trosky (even when combined with Oscar Grimes' 24, the total of 75 runs driven in by Indians first basemen was exceeded by all except Sturm and Joe Kuhel of the White Sox).

The War Years

In February 1942, Trosky told writer Gayle Hayes that he wouldn't be playing baseball at all that year. It was, he said, "for the best interest of the Cleveland club and for myself that I stay out of baseball. I have visited various doctors in the larger cities in the United States and they have not helped me. If, after resting this year, I find that I am better, perhaps I'll try to be reinstated. If I don't get better, then my major league career is over. I have asked the Cleveland club to place me on the voluntarily retired list."[8] Trosky spent 1942 on his farm in Iowa. World War II was in full bloom, and baseball contributed its share of warriors. Bob Feller went into the Navy, Joe DiMaggio and Hank Greenberg the

Army, and Ted Williams took to the air as a Marine Corps fighter pilot. Trosky stayed home, buried his brother Victor, devoured news of the war, produced food on his farm, and waited for a call from the draft board. He was a decent farmer, averaging production of over 90 bushels of corn per acre in the days before the advent of modern farming technology, and his farm—307 acres south of Walford, Iowa—provided a five percent return per year. Operated in shares with neighbor Walter Erger, it was certainly enough to support his family, even without baseball.[9] By December, though, Trosky "intimated that he [was] ready to give the game another whirl after a year in retirement."[10]

The Indians approached the Yankees about a deal to send Trosky to the Bronx, but it never came to pass. Ed Barrow made several offers to the Indians for Trosky, but

> Four different developments stood in the way of a deal.... First, the exorbitant demands of the Cleveland club. We could not possibly give up the men Alva Bradley wanted. Not for a player who might turn out physically unfit. Then there was the problem of Trosky getting a release from the farm division of the Manpower Commission. The third ... involved medical examinations concerning Hal's headaches, and last, we ran into his desire to be traded to either Chicago or Detroit, so that he could play close to ... his home.[11]

Hal Junior and Jimmy, evidently studying their father's baseball glove (*Cleveland Press* Collection, Michael Schwartz Library, Cleveland State University).

In 1943, with Lorraine pregnant with daughter Mary Kay, Trosky worked in the Amana refrigeration plant in addition to farming. His new calling was to create war supplies and support President Roosevelt's "Work or Fight" dictum. Baseball naturally faded in importance for a bit, but was never too far from Trosky's mind. Lorraine recalled times in their Iowa home, surreptitiously watching her husband as he sat glued to the radio— almost as if he could watch the game through the announcers' words—while the games were broadcast, and watching tears of frustration slip down his face while he listened to the various broadcasters describe the play of his former teammates.[12]   He ached, from the bottom of his heart, to play baseball, and he resolved that 1944 would find him in either an Army uniform or a baseball one.

James ("Jimmy"), Hal Senior and Hal Junior in Iowa, probably in 1942 (*Cleveland Press* Collection, Michael Schwartz Library, Cleveland State University).

Back in Cleveland, Franklin Lewis began a column with the lead "Trosky is a Chump," and he blamed the player for many of the woes that had befallen the Cleveland franchise. Trosky, Lewis claimed, didn't really want to return to Cleveland.

Part of the problem, alluded to by Lewis, was Trosky's monstrous 1936 season. The numbers the slugger put up in that year, his third in the majors, raised expectations beyond those which any mortal could meet. Cleveland wanted Babe Ruth's second coming. Anyone less was bound to disappoint. Lewis, naturally, did not bother to expand on the impact of the leg problems Trosky had suffered, or of the migraines which caused his lapse of vision and hitting production and which, in turn, caused the fans to jeer and thus created stress that resulted in more headaches, stomach problems and the like. No, in Franklin Lewis' world, Hal Trosky could never again suit up for the Indians.

The feeling was mutual.

Trosky worked out for the White Sox in early 1943 and, by November, the Indians had sold his contract to Chicago for $15,000. Instantly some of Trosky's burden lifted. True, the White Sox were no dynasty, and Jimmie Dykes was compelled to work managerial miracles every time the team won a game, but it would be a fresh start in a city much closer to home.

❖9❖

White Sox Years

In March 1944, the Army officially reclassified Trosky from "2C," or "deferred for agriculture," to "4F," ultimately unsuitable for military service due to his history of migraine headaches. Despite the promising results from a treatment protocol of vitamin B-1 shots, the Army wasn't in the business of taking that type of chance. Trosky appealed the decision, strongly desiring the chance to serve, especially if baseball was off the table. After three days of re-evaluation, the Army doctors stood by their judgment.

The White Sox took advantage of the Army's loss. On March 23, Trosky reported to White Sox spring training in French Lick, Indiana. Due to national travel restrictions imposed by World War II, Commissioner Landis ordered all 16 teams to hold spring training north of the Mason-Dixon Line and east of the Mississippi River.[1] The month of March in Indiana is generally just as miserable as it sounds, at least in terms of spring training for baseball. When weather failed to cooperate, the practices moved indoors at the French Lick Springs Hotel. The infielders and outfielders did their basic work in the hotel auditorium, with a dirt stage rigged to supply natural footing for the pitchers in their spikes. For the catcher's backstop there was a line of mattresses.[2] Every American was sacrificing for the war effort, and Chicago baseball teams had to feel some pain as well.

The newest White Sox player told reporters: "I'm glad to be able to give baseball a try again. And I hope I can do the Sox some good." When asked about the Army's summary of his health, he added, "I didn't expect to be rejected. I'd have been glad to do my part along with all the other fellows who have gone. But the doctors know their business and they know what the Army wants."[3]

Trosky was happily reunited with coach Bing Miller, the same man who'd offered contract advice back in 1930, but he played baseball in 1944 like a man with great talent who had been out of the game for two seasons. In April he recorded several multi-RBI games, but showed no consistency. His play was marked by alternating series of solid games with mediocre performances. At the end of the first month of the season he was hitting only .267 with five home runs. By the end of May he was hitting .240 but had driven in only 14 runs in 121 at-bats and was reduced to platooning with Eddie Cornett at first base. There were flashes of the old Trosky power, of

A 1944 shot of Trosky in the on-deck circle with his new team, the Chicago White Sox (*Cleveland Press* Collection, Michael Schwartz Library, Cleveland State University).

Prince Hal, but they seemed to fade just short of being a significant help to the team.

On August 15, facing Bill Zuber at Yankee Stadium, Trosky hit a sixth-inning drive high and long into deep right field only to watch the right fielder make a leaping catch against the wall. That episode was a microcosm of his entire season: Good, but not quite good enough.

One of Trosky's teammates on the White Sox was Ralph Hodgin, a third baseman who led Chicago in hitting in 1944 with a .295 average. In an interview in 1994, he discussed how difficult home runs were to come by in Chicago. The right field fence at Comiskey was 352 feet from home plate, but the wind always blew in and kept most fly balls in play. On the rare days when the wind was blowing out, rain often followed and resulted in cancellation of the scheduled game.

Hodgin remembered Hal Trosky as a "pretty nice guy, always friendly and such." Trosky's headaches were occasionally extreme, Hodgin recalled, sometimes so brutal that even the quiet Trosky would complain about them, but the White Sox players never held that against him.[4]

Headaches notwithstanding, Trosky still managed ten home runs in 1944, which was enough to lead the team. Lorraine and the four children now lived full-time in Cedar Rapids, commuting to Chicago only occasionally for a game or two. At the end of 1944, with the White Sox in seventh place after winning only 71 games, Trosky called it quits again. He headed home for some hunting and farming and to await another possible call-up to support the war effort.

However, 1945 found him working again at the Amana Refrigeration plant. The longer course of B-1 vitamin shots and a significant reduction in his daily intake of dairy products helped partially control the headaches, but it was cruel irony that an Iowa dairy farmer was allergic to the very stuff his animals produced and he consumed so frequently in order to maintain his athletic frame. The treatments, along with three years of emotional distance from his time with the Indians, helped lessen the migraines considerably, and the end of the war presented Trosky with one more opportunity to recapture the thunder in his bat.

The White Sox offered Trosky a salary raise to play another year for Chicago. "Trosky needs about a year to get back into stride," said manager Jimmie Dykes. "He's hit as many as 42 homeruns in a season, and there's no reason he can't get 25 a year, once he finds his stride."[5] The Pale Hose hadn't been able to find a regular first baseman in 1945, after giving both Kerby Farrell and Bill Nogel ample opportunity to win the job, so the prospect of Trosky's big bat reawakening was too enticing to ignore. Even with the falloff in 1944, his lifetime batting average was still .305, and he remained what one writer termed "potentially the hardest-hitting first baseman in the American League."[6]

Unfortunately for both the slugger and the White Sox, the dream had been closer to a nightmare. Trosky's season opened on April 16, and he went 0-for-his-first-two-games before posting a three-hit effort in St. Louis. After that game, though, he managed only five hits for the rest of the month and started May with a less-than-robust .182 batting average and only one home run. Nine strikeouts and six walks summarized his first month back and underscored how much his batting eye had atrophied. There were a number of factors contributing to his malaise. First was the reality that he'd played only one season in the preceding four and that rust was unavoidable. Also, with the war now over, the full complement of major leaguers were back in the game; instead of facing wartime replacement pitchers like 39-year-old journeyman Luke Hamlin or Jesse Flores, he was again stepping in against Bob Feller or Spud Chandler. Additionally, the defense behind those pitchers was again of true major league caliber.

But at the core, Trosky was trying to come back to an elite level at one of the most difficult tasks in sport. In May he appeared in only 11 games, and his batting average never crested .200. June provided a bit of a turnaround, as he showed flashes of the old Trosky, but they were just that, flashes. Nine multi-hit games helped his average climb to a respectable .269, but he never found his consistent power stroke.

The White Sox finished the year only two games out of the first division, but were 30 games behind the champion Red Sox. Trosky hit only .254 with two home runs and 31 RBI. Despite Chicago's offer of $25,000 to suit up again in 1947 (he was only 34 years old), Trosky knew it was time to hang up the spikes for good. "One day," he told Maury White, "Dizzy Trout was throwing hard ones and I asked to be taken out. Then [another time] the pitcher threw to first on a pickoff and hit me in the belly. I didn't even see the ball. I knew it was time to get out."[7]

After 228 home runs and 1,012 runs batted in, Trosky bid farewell to the game he loved so much. This time, however, he did so with no regrets and with no sense of promise unfulfilled. A brief look at Trosky's career reveals just how powerful he'd been before the headaches and injuries began to exact their collective toll.

Hal Trosky logged 1,096 total bases in his first three full seasons, or 470 games counting the 11 in 1933, an extraordinarily high total regardless of baseball era. In terms of pure "counting" statistics (as opposed to "rate" stats), by the time Trosky had played three full major league seasons, he had accrued 606 hits that included 104 home runs, and driven in 425 runs. While certainly not comparing the athletes across eras, but merely using their numbers for a sort of rough analog, through 2015 Nationals outfield star Bryce Harper collected 947 total bases in 50 more games, to go with 97 homers and 248 RBI. In Mike

Trout's first 493 games, he rang up 1,029 total bases with 98 home runs and 307 RBI.

Again, those comparisons are across eras, with so many conditions having changed, but it is easy to imagine how much money Trosky might have earned had he not played in the pre-free agency days and during a worldwide economic depression. The point is that Trosky was even more the slugger that Cy Slapnicka had envisioned when he signed the boy in 1930.

Hal Trosky finished in the top ten in American League MVP voting twice (seventh after his 1934 rookie season and tenth in 1936), and in the top thirty in 1938 and 1939. Four times he finished in the top ten in the American League in batting average, and his career .302 mark is still 178th on the all-time major league list. He had over 200 hits in a single season in 1934 and 1936, and finished in the top ten in RBI and total bases five times each. He was also in the top ten in AL homers six times, topped by his second-place finish with 42 home runs in that amazing 1936 campaign.

His ubiquity in the Cleveland Indians' record book is significant. His .644 slugging average in 1936 remains the seventh-best in team history, and his career .551 mark is fourth behind Manny Ramirez, Albert Belle, and Jim Thome, and ahead of Averill, Shoeless Joe Jackson, and Tris Speaker. He is sixth in career total bases (his 405 in 1936 is still the franchise single season record), ninth in doubles and fifth in home runs. With the exception of Manny Ramirez's 1999 campaign, in which he drove in 165 runs, no Indian has had a better RBI year than Trosky in 1936, and he is fourth on the franchise career list with 911 runs driven in.

He is also fourth on the Indians' career list with 556 extra-base hits and had the second- and fourth-best single seasons in that capacity (96 in 1936 and 89 in 1934). Finally, he is twelfth all-time in batting average (.313) and seventh in OPS (on-base percentage plus slugging average, used as a rough gauge of a player's overall offensive value) with a mark of .930.

Including his 1944 season, he led his teams seven times in home runs. Trosky homered in nine different parks and off 112 different pitchers during his career, and his most frequent victims were Tommy Bridges and Bump Hadley with ten apiece. Of his 228 home runs, 106 were hit on the road, and 122 at home. No one, with the exception of Earl Averill, hit more home runs at Cleveland's League Park.

Applying the 162-game-season template to his numbers, he would have averaged 188 hits, scored 100 runs, hit 27 homers, and driven in 122 runs. Those feats, along with an average of 40 doubles, a slugging average of .522 and an OPS of .892.

Finally, with 228, he hit more homers than any other player hailing from Iowa. By any reasonable standard, Hal Trosky's career was a success, and his ability to punish a baseball was unquestionable. His streak of eight consecutive Opening Day starts for the Indians is still the longest in team history. He was, and is, an all-time Cleveland Indian, and is honored with a plaque in Progressive Field's Heritage Park. In 1965 he was inducted into the Iowa Sports and the Cedar Rapids Baseball Halls of Fame.

Later Years

On February 4, 1947, the White Sox formally released Trosky and simultaneously signed him as one of their Midwest scouts.[8] Between 1947–1950, he often scoured the tiny towns of eastern Iowa looking for "the next Feller" or "the next Trosky," while still maintaining his

Hal Trosky's final major league team, the 1946 Chicago White Sox. Trosky is third from the left in the back row. His final year in baseball was also the first post-war season, in which many of the stars that had been on active duty in 1944 had returned to the diamond. It was also the final year of segregated baseball—Jackie Robinson, Larry Doby, Hank Thompson and Willard "Home Run" Brown would all wear major league uniforms in 1947.

family farm near Norway. He also worked occasionally for Amana Refrigeration. Although Trosky had enough service to qualify for a pension of sorts, the various jobs helped the player inside him ease through the transition from the game of baseball to the business of life.

There was always baseball, though, and Trosky continued to find interesting ways to stay involved. In 1947, his first full year following retirement from his playing career, Trosky's old wartime employer, Amana Refrigeration, sponsored a semi-pro team in the thriving National Baseball Congress. Using their close proximity to the University of Iowa and its baseball team, the Freezers recruited Hawkeyes shortstop Robert Primrose, future major leaguer Jack Dittmer, and one Emlen "Gremlin" Tunnell. To fill the coach and managerial roles, Amana hired Trosky for the tournament season.

Dittmer later played 695 major league games at second base for the Boston/Milwaukee Braves and the Detroit Tigers, but in Tunnell the Freezers had a future Hall of Famer. In Tunnell's case, though, that recognition came on the gridiron as a star over a 14-year career with the New York "football" Giants and the Green Bay Packers. He is credited with hitting one of the longest home runs ever at Cedar Rapids' Daniels Park, and in 1949—in a brief five-game stint with the Cedar Rapids Rockets of the Class C Central Association (CENA) drilled five hits in 18 at-bats.[9] More importantly, his appearances marked the first by any black player in the CENA and in the state of Iowa (since the days of Keokuk's Bud Fowler in the 1880s). Two years after Jackie Robinson's debut, the Central Association finally had its first Negro player, and he wore a Cedar Rapids uniform.

Tunnell, of course, broke yet another barrier when, in 1967, he became the first black player inducted into the Pro Football Hall of Fame after a career highlighted by 79 interceptions and 2,209 punt return yards. He was the greatest athlete on an outstanding Freezers baseball team.

The "Amana Freezers" ran up a 27–2 record in winning almost every Iowa tournament they entered, split a two-game set with the Cedar Rapids Manufacturers-and-Jobbers All Stars (featuring several former professional players), and just missed going to the semi-pro World Series that year in Wichita, Kansas. The fact that the team was primarily local, without imported talent from outside the region, made them a big draw wherever they played, and literally thousands filled the stands when the Freezers won the Waterloo (IA) District Semi-Pro tournament in July. It was an impressive turnout for the time and a testament to both the players and their coach.

Trosky finally left the Sox for good in 1950 and, after farming for a few more years, took up full-time agricultural real estate sales (trying to help people "buy the farm," no less) around Cedar Rapids. With four growing children, and all three boys excelling in sports, it was a fortuitously lucrative decision. His income, coupled with Lorraine's frugality, enabled the family to continue to prosper and grow. He and Lorraine also became even more active working with their church. They were always devout Catholics (he even gave up swearing later in life, but retained his sole vice of chewing tobacco in later years) and contributed ample time and money to the community they loved so deeply.

By 1970, farming was a secondary occupation. He had some cattle, in addition to the fields, but his farm had shrunk from 500 acres to 100 when he retired. "I don't see too much baseball ... mostly it's by TV now.... I used to do a lot of work with American League teams here,"[10] but in his sixties he had started to slow down. Trosky suffered a heart attack in early 1978, and by 1979 was moving around only with the support of a cane. Son Jim Trosky remembered that period:

> I was not living in Cedar Rapids at the time. I was working for United Air Lines and living in the Chicago area. I was told this by Mom and I will tell you to the best of my recollection: Dad was sent home from the hospital basically to die. I remember that because I was there with Mom and the other kids when the decision was made. His heart had been ravaged so badly by a virus that to repair it was not an option and they could do no more for him at the hospital. For several months he lived at home and [sisters] Esther and Annette would come to help Mom take care of him. One day, out of the blue, he got up, walked into the kitchen, got the keys to the car, walked out, got in it and drove down to the farm south of town just like nothing was wrong with him. His cardiologist said it was impossible ... that there was not enough of his heart left to even keep him alive. A miracle? We think so. For approximately nine months this went on.... Dad would visit people, witness about God to them, spend time just messing around at the farm and ... unfortunately, in the process, ending up, what we all believe, was giving most of his baseball mementoes away. To who ... we wish we knew, probably just people who came down to visit him and asked for them. His Cleveland uniform plus many other mementoes are still out there ... somewhere. Sad, but if he was happy doing that then I guess we should be happy as well. One day he just fell down and died at home ... that fast. Dad and Mom both were tremendous influences on all of us. Dad's integrity in all matters and Mom's loving ways have been our heritage.... I was the Second Officer

9. *White Sox Years*

on a DC-6 out of New York that the Yankees had chartered to take the team somewhere to play a league game. That was back in 1964. The Captain mentioned on the PA that the son of Hal Trosky was part of their crew. Mel Allen came up to the cockpit to meet me and to tell me that my Dad was one of the finest gentlemen he had ever met in his life. Just out of the blue ... nothing solicited. You can imagine my pride at that moment.[11]

One May morning Lorraine looked out her window, and in a moment of panic saw her husband's cane lying on the ground near their car. With a mixture of relief and fury, she looked further and saw Hal trying to push the car out of a small pothole in the driveway. She "raised the roof" with him, and he contritely promised to act his age and he

Hal Trosky and his first baseball mentors, sisters Annette (left) and Esther in their later years, circa 1978 (courtesy Susan Volz).

more careful. Of course, he'd always been one to do whatever he felt he had to, only later "fessing up" to his wondering wife. This time, though, he assured her that he would obey.

On June 18, 1979, Lorraine was in the kitchen of their apartment, putting away the dinner dishes, when she heard a loud crash in the hallway. She came out to find Hal collapsed on the floor. He was already gone. The doctors said the heart attack was so massive that Trosky was dead by the time he hit the floor. He was officially pronounced Dead-On-Arrival at Mercy Hospital in Cedar Rapids, and is buried in St Michael's Cemetery on a hillside overlooking his hometown of Norway, Iowa.

Hal Trosky, Junior

Hal Junior was nine when his parents moved him from Norway to Cedar Rapids in order for him to attend St. Patrick's High School. It was just a short drive from the family farm, but since Norway could not offer a parochial secondary education, Hal and Lorraine took matters into their own hands. The move proved providential, as Junior was nearly as talented an athlete as his father.

The boy worked, of course, including some part-time employment for the railroad as a laborer, but he still found time to excel on the diamond for St. Patrick's. Under head coach Joe Kenney, Hal never endured a losing season. As the boy's hitting skill became more widely known, the number of scouts at his games grew. *The Sporting News* (June 9, 1954) reported that 12 major-league clubs were scouting Hal, attracted by his .667 batting average as a senior, his corner-infield skills, and his stellar performance as the top hitter on the Cedar Rapids American Legion team, a squad that had recently won the Iowa state title.

Hal began receiving offers from major league teams. Hal Senior, who had spent some time as a scout for the White Sox, screened the various offers and, according to *The Sporting News*, Hal Junior told the local papers that he planned to attend the University of Notre Dame in the fall unless there was an offer "too good to turn down."[12]

With so many interested scouts, and given his father's baseball prominence, Hal had met various team executives during the recruiting process. He instantly liked Charlie Comiskey, Jr., the White Sox owner, from their first meeting, and in 1954 he signed a contract with White Sox scout Johnny Mostil. The White Sox sent him to the Colorado Springs Sky Sox of the Class A Western League, where manager Eddie Stewart was to evaluate him for two weeks. After that, the organization told Hal, he would be placed at an appropriate level.

Manager Stewart put Trosky in the starting lineup right away, playing first base, and on June 22, 1954, he hit a home run in his first at-bat. In his second game he was hit on the left hand by a pitch and three fingers were broken. He spent three weeks on the disabled list.

After returning to the lineup, Trosky kept his batting average just over .300 until he was injured again, in a game in Denver. "I was doing the splits, fielding a throw. The runner, Rocky Ippolito, ran into my left hamstring and tore it up pretty badly," he said. "The next day, after consulting with the White Sox, the general manager at Colorado Springs told me they wanted me to continue to play. I did, and by the end of the season my batting average dropped about 60 points." By the end of his first year in professional baseball, his average had fallen to .252, but the 59 games only seemed to whet Chicago's appetite.

During the off-season, on Valentine's Day 1955, Trosky married Ellen Mae Gibson in St. Patrick's Church in Cedar Rapids. As his parents had, Hal and Ella Mae eventually had four children, two sons and two daughters. Trosky labored as a sheet-metal worker that first off-season, but earned his insurance license the following year.

He opened 1955 with the Superior Blues of the Class C Northern League, and almost immediately he was injured again. As he fielded a throw that was low and up the baseline, the runner came inside the line and ran into the forearm on his glove hand. The result was a quarter-sized bone chip on his left elbow that made him unable to flex his arm. After 40 games, his second season was over, and he returned to Iowa to rehabilitate the arm. His orthopedic physician advised him that surgery might permanently restrict his arm movement, and instead recommended that he spend the off-season exercising daily with a five-gallon bucket of sand.

Trosky was disciplined in his therapy. By the first day of 1956 spring training, he had regained more than 90 percent of his flexibility and range of motion. He was invited to spring training with the White Sox, and though he was batting .345, a coach approached him one morning. "Have you ever thought about pitching?" the coach asked.

"We think that the little restriction that you have remaining in your left arm will keep you from hitting big-league pitching. But we've noticed that everything you throw has natural movement on it and we want you to try pitching." Trosky was 6-feet-3 and weighed 205 pounds, so size was not an issue for the White Sox.

Hal's father had advised him to try anything the big-league club suggested, within reason, so he worked as a pitcher the rest of the spring. When he returned to Superior, it was as a side-arm pitcher, but White Sox pitching coach Ray Berres told him that he'd never get big-league hitters out throwing side-arm. The right-handed Trosky changed to a three-quarter delivery and used his fastball and "nickle curve" (today called a slider) to earn nine wins and post a 3.95 earned-run average for Duluth-Superior in his first season on the mound. At that point, Hal's career was a mirror image of his father's: Hal Senior had begun as a pitcher and moved to first base. In 1957 Trosky was promoted to the Davenport (Iowa) Davsox of the Class B Three-I League, and lowered his ERA to 3.66 while logging a 14–10 record. His progress was so dramatic that *The Sporting News* speculated over the winter that he might crack the Chicago pitching staff in 1958.

Trosky stayed with Chicago until the end of spring training in 1958, but the team (one year away from winning the American League pennant) had sufficient depth and assigned him instead to Indianapolis of the Triple-A American Association to start the season. After some organizational maneuvering, Hal found himself again playing with Colorado Springs in June. When the Sky Sox came to Des Moines for a series, Hal Senior and Lorraine drove there from Cedar Rapids to spend a few days with their son.

Hal Trosky, Sr., had always been extraordinarily busy during his playing career and had endured all types of pressure, both on and off the field. The only pressure he couldn't take, it turned out, was watching his eldest son play once the latter had turned professional. Hal Junior (or Hoot Junior, as he was called in professional baseball circles) had pitched nine innings in the game before the team arrived in Des Moines, so the elder Troskys felt assured that they could visit without their son being at risk to pitch.

On Father's Day 1958, Colorado Springs and Des Moines were halfway through a doubleheader when Hal and Lorraine decided to head back to Cedar Rapids in order to get home before dark. After

Hal Trosky, Jr., in his Chicago White Sox uniform in 1958. Now grown, the son of the former Indians and White Sox first baseman, Hal Trosky, Jr., was a widely recruited slugging star while in high school in Iowa. He became a pitcher after a devastating injury in the minor leagues, and made it to Chicago for two big-league appearances in 1958.

their goodbyes, and with his parents safely on the road, Colorado Springs manager Frank Scalzi asked Hal if he could pitch the nightcap because the scheduled starter had injured himself while warming up. Trosky took the ball that afternoon and, while his parents were navigating Iowa State Route 30 back to Cedar Rapids, threw the only no-hitter of his life. His parents were thrilled when Hal called them that night, but Hal Senior was just as happy that he'd missed the stress of the game.

Hal Junior posted a 13–9 record in the minors that year, and in September he was called up to the White Sox. He made his major league debut on September 25, against the Detroit Tigers, when he relieved Stover McIlwain in the fifth and pitched a scoreless inning. Trosky pitched one inning and picked up the victory after a late White Sox rally brought an 11–4 win. Three days later, on the last day of the regular season, Trosky pitched two innings in relief against the Kansas City Athletics and got the victory, even though he gave up three runs. Those three innings pitched proved to be his entire major league career.

His stint in the Kansas City game was a bit unusual. SABR member

Norman Macht recounted it the *Baseball Research Journal*: After Trosky pitched a scoreless fifth inning, Chicago scored three runs in the last of the fifth and took a 6–1 lead. "Taking the mound for the sixth," Macht wrote,

> Trosky looked around his infield and took comfort from the steadying presence of [Nellie] Fox. Then a rare series of events occurred. Three ground balls were hit to Fox. Two went through his legs and one bounced off his chest. All three were scored as hits. Trosky walked a couple, and Suitcase Simpson, who had hit Trosky hard in the minors, roped one into center field for the only solid hit of the inning, and three runs were in. In the last of the sixth Jim Rivera batted for Trosky and struck out. Bob Shaw finished up. The win was credited to Trosky. He was twenty-two the next day. He never pitched another big-league inning.[13]

The next year, 1959 Trosky stayed with the White Sox until the final day of spring training, but was again sent to Indianapolis. After a 3–2 start, and pitching in eight straight games, he was sent to the Memphis Chickasaws of the Double-A Southern Association, playing for his father's old teammate, now Memphis manager, Luke Appling. As late as 2012, Trosky said he still had no idea why he was sent down.

He had developed some calcification in his pitching shoulder, which may have prompted the transfer, but one night opposing coach Mel Parnell saw Trosky's throwing motion and diagnosed him on the spot. Parnell, an outstanding left-handed pitcher for the Boston Red Sox in his day, had suffered a similar malady and cured it with radiation treatments. He recommended the treatment to Hal. It included visiting a physician who happened to practice in Memphis. After a series of the radiation treatments, the shoulder healed.

Now healthy, Trosky was recalled to Indianapolis over both his and manager Appling's protests. Ellen was pregnant with son Gregg, so Hal drove the family back to Iowa and then flew out to join the team. The year finished without event, and the Troskys looked forward to 1960.

In the fall of 1959, Ellen became pregnant again, now with daughter Tracy, and doctors discovered unexpected complications during a prenatal visit. There were blood compatibility issues between Ellen and her unborn child, so Hal remained home (without a contract) until he could be sure that both would be healthy. The clearance did not come until Tracy was born in late July. Except for a one-game stint with

Nashville of the Southern Association, Hal's chances had passed for the season.

While awaiting Tracy's birth, Trosky played with Iowa Manufacturing in the local Manufacturers & Jobbers league in Cedar Rapids, so he was in shape for 1961. When several contracts arrived from the White Sox, however, he returned them unsigned.

While Trosky was in Nashville, his manager, former New York Yankees pitching coach Jim Turner, had told him that he'd have been in the major leagues "two years ago" with any other team. That morsel

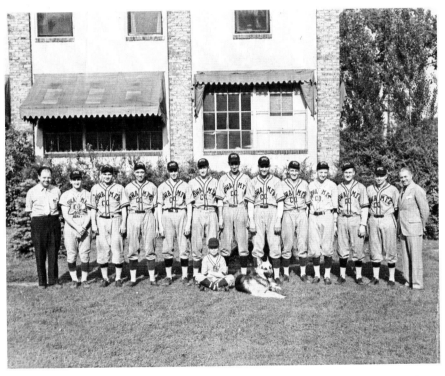

A photograph of the "Iowa Manufacturing" company team that competed in the Cedar Rapids' Manufacturers and Jobbers League between 1941 and 1962. The "M&J", as it was abbreviated, was home to a number of talented players, including major leaguers Hal Trosky, Jr., Clarence "Junior" Walter, Orie Arntzen, Dick Rozek and Bill Zuber, and Negro National League star Art Pennington. The owner of Iowa Manufacturing, Howard Hall, is pictured at the far right. Hall was a visionary force in sustaining the high caliber of baseball in eastern Iowa.

of awareness, coupled with his own assessment, the fact that several other teams had been in contact with the White Sox seeking to acquire him, and that Chuck Comiskey no longer owned the team, had convinced Trosky that he had no future in Chicago.

The White Sox asked if his contracts were being returned due to a salary issue. No, Hal assured them, all he wanted was his release. "A year and a half later they were offered what I thought was a generous amount for me," Hal told Norman Macht. "They turned it down. Every spring for three years scouts came around and wanted to see me throw. They still wanted me. After that I'd been out too long. Physically I could come back but I couldn't get mentally and emotionally ready again. I don't know what the club's thinking was. I guess somebody up there didn't like me." Eventually the team stopped sending contracts, but did not comply with Trosky's request for a release for more than a decade, until 1972, after he had turned 36 years old.

Trosky had earned his insurance license in October 1955, and he had developed his clientele over each off-season since then. In 1961 he became a full-time insurance agent in Cedar Rapids, and worked for several firms over the years before opening his own agency in the 1980s. He owned the agency until his death in 2013, the end coming after a brief bout with cancer.

Hal's eldest son was the only one who eventually entered professional baseball as a competitor. Second son Jim enjoyed a career as a pilot for United Air Lines, and son Lynn moved to California and opened his own hair styling business in Carmel-by-the-sea. Lynn's son Nate has carved out an extremely successful career in baseball, most recently as founder and owner of Trosky Baseball in California. Nate was an NAIA All-American player at Hawaii Pacific University and by 1995 was working as a scout and coach for a number of organizations. In addition to coaching for two independent league teams, he has coached for the German National team and also scouts for the Milwaukee Brewers. Trosky Baseball hosts showcase events, provides scouting and evaluation of youth players, and generally carries on the Trosky family baseball legacy.

Further out on the family tree, Hal's nephew, Robert Primrose, played at the University of Iowa and for the 1947 Amana Freezers before joining the U.S. Air Force. Robert flew F-80s in Korea during that conflict, and eventually flew the U-2 surveillance aircraft during the Cuban Missile Crisis. He died in a training accident in 1964. Robert's brother Harold also played at the University of Iowa before entering a coaching career that culminated in his induction into the American Baseball Coaches Association Hall of Fame, selection as National High School Coach of the Year, and recipient of ABCA's prestigious "Lefty Gomez Award."

In addition to Robert and Harold, Trosky's sister Esther (one of his early barn coaches while growing up) had two daughters, Gayle Holt and Susan Volz. Susan, in turn, had a grandson, Nate Frese, who made it all the way to the AAA Iowa Cubs before leaving baseball to farm for a living, and all three of her sons played for the Norway High School team during the glory years of 1965–1991. It is almost impossible to shake the Trosky family tree and not dislodge a few baseballs.

The Hal Trosky story is far more than the biography of a single man. He was by all accounts a wonderful human being, father, husband, friend, and baseball player. His story, though, necessarily intersects with the larger histories of baseball, of Ohio and Iowa, of cities like Cleveland and Cedar Rapids, and of small towns like Norway. Hal Trosky's life always returned to his heartland home in Iowa.

Billy Hoffer and Belden Hill effectively established and professionalized the game of baseball in Cedar Rapids. Those men, in turn, watched and encouraged Earl Whitehill, Bing Miller, and Hal Trosky, among others, who then put the city on the baseball map. Hal Trosky, in turn, watched and encouraged young players, notably Bruce Kimm and Mike Boddicker, in their successes. Kimm played or managed at just about every level, and on every stage, imaginable, from informal "fast rubber" contests as a boy in Norway through major league All-Star Games, a World Series, and as manager of the Cubs.

Baseball was, is, and likely always will be part of the DNA of Cedar Rapids and of eastern Iowa. It is a natural pairing, and it is impossible to tell the story of one without describing the other. In other words, it is similar to a marriage that has lasted for 150 years, yet remains as solid as ever. And at the heart of the heartland's game, at least in eastern Iowa, Hal Trosky's shadow will always exist somewhere in the background.

Appendix
Trosky's Most Memorable Games

Over the course of a career, every baseball player will play in a few games that remain etched in memory, and those memories become stories later in life. Over time, those stories are embellished—unintentionally or otherwise—until the feats gain the status of myth. Trosky played in 1,347 games over his 11-year major league career, and a few of those have become stories told and retold over the years, some to the point of complete inaccuracy. What follows are actual accounts of a few of his most notable games, including his encounter with Babe Ruth, his first three-homer game in 1934, the doubleheader in which he batted from both sides of the plate, and a few others. The accounts have been fused from newspaper accounts of the day along with the outstanding information available at retrosheet.org.

The last game surveyed, Trosky's final big-league tilt, is especially interesting in that he enjoyed one of the best afternoons of his White Sox tenure, and then sat on the bench the following day. It was, somehow, appropriate.

Trosky Meets the Babe—September 17, 1933

In many baseball biographies, game accounts tend to focus on the more successful encounters, not on the ones that highlight failure. Yet baseball is a game of failure that is only occasionally, and happily, punctuated by success. Failure is fair game in the story of any player's life. Fans attending this particular game, as it played out, saw a very young rookie from Iowa go 0-for-4 with four strikeouts against Lefty Gomez.

The game, however, was one that Hal Trosky remembered and recounted his entire life, and one of the first he'd talk about when fans might ask about memories of his playing days. Not only was he able to laugh at himself and his four strikeouts but, as noted earlier, the experience of playing alongside the Great Bambino was one of his great memories of his entire career.

The first game of the Sunday twin bill saw the Indians fall to New York, 3–2, in a one hour and 41-minute contest in which both starting pitchers, Russ Van Atta and Monte Pearson, went the distance. After a quick breather in the dugout, the teams retook the field for game two. This was one of the marquee pitching matchups of the day, with Mel Harder—en route to winning the American League ERA title— facing the All-Star Game starter for the American League, Lefty Gomez, in the Bronx. Bill Summers was the plate umpire for the game, and George Hildebrand and Bill McGowan staffed first and third bases.

Gomez mowed down the Indians' Dick Porter, Bill Knickerbocker, and Earl Averill 1–2–3 in the top of the first, and Harder responded by setting the Yankees down with no hits in the bottom of the inning. Trosky led off Cleveland's second with a three-pitch strikeout. Odell Hale attempted to bunt for a base hit but failed, as Bill Dickey's throw to Gehrig easily beat him. With two outs, an intriguing hitter stepped into the box. In an interesting lineup twist, Walter Johnson started pitcher Wes Ferrell in left field.

Ferrell was already a tremendous pitcher. He won 193 games over a 15-year big league career with Cleveland, Boston, Washington and New York before finishing in the National League. He made 20-plus season wins six times and 25 wins twice. In his best season, 1935, he won 25 games, completed 31 and tossed 322⅓ innings while finishing second in league MVP voting. But he was exceptionally gifted with a bat in his hands, perhaps the best-hitting pitcher (after Ruth) of all time. In that same 1935 season, he rapped out 52 hits in 150 at-bats for a .347 batting average. Seven of those hits were home runs, and he struck out only 16 times. Wes' brother Rick played 19 years as a major league catcher, and despite Wes having ten more career homers than his younger sibling, it was Rick who was elected to the Hall of Fame.

It was not a stretch for Johnson to look around the dugout and decide that Wes Ferrell's bat was too valuable to leave on the bench. That so stipulated, he whiffed against Gomez to end the inning.

The Yankees managed a walk and a Bill Dickey single in the bottom of the second, but Gomez grounded into a double play to end the threat. In the top of the third, the Indians again went down in order to give Gomez a perfect pass through the Tribe's lineup. In the Yankees' third, with two out, Trosky was playing deep behind first base when Babe Ruth hit a scorching line drive down the line that carried the rookie's mitt almost halfway into right field. After retrieving the glove, the rookie had to sift through the conflicting emotions of awe, in the presence of a living legend, and of fear, in the form of Lou Gehrig striding to the plate. Gehrig represented an even greater hazard to Trosky's well-being than the Bambino, because Ruth generally hit high, arcing fly balls, while Gehrig could rip a vicious line drive off any pitch.

By doctrine, Trosky was supposed to cover first with second base open, but against Gehrig the only chance to reel in a hard drive was in playing farther back on the outfield grass. The Babe must have divined Trosky's fielding dilemma, because he whispered out of the side of his mouth, "Don't worry about holding me on, kid. I ain't going no place. Just drop back a little and play it safe. If he hit one at you up here, it would take your head off."[1] Trosky backed off and, true to his word, Ruth stood just a few feet from first and waited. It certainly wasn't that big a deal to the Babe, but Trosky never forgot the small kindness, and he later had the glove bronzed for his personal collection.

That encounter with Ruth stayed with Trosky for the rest of his life. Decades later, in 1976, he responded to the request of a fan and autograph seeker simply named Ed, writing the following on a 3×5 notecard:

Dear Ed.

My biggest thrill in baseball was to play against "Babe" Ruth and to be lucky enough to play Major League Baseball.

Sincerely, Hal Trosky

In Cleveland on that afternoon, though, the game tension continued through the fourth inning, which ended with another three-pitch whiff by Trosky, followed by a Yankees run in the bottom of the inning, and into the bottom of the fifth. It was then that Ruth took over. Gordon Cobbledick wrote: "All by himself Mr. Ruth spoiled an otherwise pleasant and potentially profitable afternoon for the Indians."[2] Former Indian Joe Sewell walked, and Ruth hammered his 30th home run of the year. It was all the offense Gomez would need.

The Yankees built their lead without a response from the Indians. Trosky struck out again in the seventh to end the inning, and Cleveland finally got on the board in the eighth when Ferrell walked and scored on a Frankie Pytlak double. Almost as significantly, especially to the 18,000 or so in attendance, was that Pytlak's hit was the first given up by Gomez on the day. That hit seemed to wake up the New York bats, as they answered with three runs in the bottom of the inning. Trosky struck out for a fourth time in the ninth, and Cleveland walked off with a 6–1 loss.

Trosky's First Big Game—May 30, 1934[3]

On May 29, in a Tuesday afternoon tilt at League Park against the White Sox, Hal Trosky knocked a two-run homer in support of starting pitcher Mel Harder and a 5–0 Indians victory. The following day, in the first game of a doubleheader against Chicago, he managed only two singles in a 12-inning loss to the visitors. In the nightcap, however, 21-year-old Hal Trosky hammered homers in three consecutive at-bats to pace a 5–4 Indians win. It was only the third time that had ever occurred at League Park, preceded by Earl Averill in 1930 and—naturally—Joe Hauser, back in 1924.

The game began innocuously enough when Chicago's "Frenchy" Bordagaray grounded out to pitcher Willis Hudlin. After Trosky's White Sox counterpart, Zeke Bonura, hit into a double play, the Indians managed only an Earl Averill single in the bottom of the inning. In Cleveland's second frame, Trosky made the second out of the inning with a lazy pop fly to second base. In the top of the fourth, the White Sox threatened after a Bonura double, but a rare double play ground ball by Luke Appling snuffed the rally.

In the bottom of the fourth, with two out and Odell Hale on first, Trosky lined a fastball over the tall right field fence, just barely inside the foul line. Hudlin settled into a groove, and put Chicago down 1–2–3 in both the fifth and sixth innings, extending his personal scoreless-innings streak to 15. In Cleveland's half of the sixth, with one out, Trosky again launched a shot off pitcher, and fellow Iowan, Les Tietje over the screen in right field, this time at least 30 feet from the pole. It was, by all accounts, even more impressive than his earlier blast, and extended the Indians' lead to four runs.

Hudlin ran into trouble in the top of the seventh. Zeke Bonura led off with another double and scored on Al Simmons' single to center field. Appling atoned for his earlier double play ball with a single to right field and moved over to second when player-manager Jimmie Dykes singled to left, scoring Simmons. After a sacrifice bunt and a pop out to Trosky at first, Dykes pinch-hit for Tietje with rookie outfielder Frenchy Uhalt (yes, another "Frenchy"—an easy moniker for any player considered to be of French descent). Uhalt promptly smote a two-run single to right and stole second before the inning ended on Frenchy Bordagaray's fly out to right field. By the time the dust had settled, the game was tied, 4–4. Interestingly, in the current (post–1990) game, Hudlin would likely have been pulled for a reliever somewhere in the midst of that five-hit, four-run inning. Johnson, however, left Willis in the game and let him work out of the trouble, perhaps trusting the offense to pick up the pitcher in the late innings. The strategy worked.

Dykes handed the ball to another right-hander, Phil Gallivan, as Tietje's relief, and the youngster set down the Tribe with just a Bill Knickerbocker single in the seventh. Hudlin returned to the mound in the eighth inning, dispatched Mule Haas and Bonura on infield grounders, and whiffed Simmons to end the frame.

With one out and the score tied in the bottom of the eighth, Trosky unloaded his longest blast of the day, and perhaps one of the longest of his career. The ball cleared the middle exit gate at League Park and flew well over 400 feet before landing all the way across Lexington Avenue. In an age before tape-measure graphics on television, it was left to reporter Gordon Cobbledick to convey the magnitude of the shot. "All three were socks that would have cleared the barrier in any park in the major leagues, but [Trosky] saved his best shot for the last. That one, soaring high over the wall in right center, smashed through the wind shield of a car parked deep in a lot on the far side of Lexington Avenue."[4]

Cleveland entered the ninth inning with a 5–4 lead, and while Hudlin gave up a leadoff single to Appling, he induced a third double-play grounder, this time off Jimmie Dykes' bat, and an easy roller to third by Boken to end the game. The game lasted only one hour and 55 minutes, despite 17 hits combined, but home plate umpire Clarence Bernard "Brick" Owens—a most apt moniker in that at age 49 he carried at least 200 pounds on a 5'10" frame—kept the pace brisk. It was Hudlin's fifth straight victory, but Trosky's power was the lead story in all of the local papers.

Trosky Switches Sides—September 15, 1935

Over the course of a Sunday afternoon doubleheader at Griffith Stadium in Washington, D.C., Hal Trosky "took a desperate way out of desperate straits ... and got away with it."[5] The two games were played between a visiting squad that was 19 games behind the first-place Tigers, and the hometown Senators, who were 28 out of the lead. It wasn't that either team was hoping to creep into contention, but there were just two weeks left in the season for pride, for each player to build a case for retaining his job in 1936, and for a few an opportunity to negotiate a tiny raise as well. Over 18,000 fans, the largest crowd since Opening Day, filled the stands to watch.[6]

To start the first game, with the seemingly ubiquitous Brick Owens again behind the plate, rookie pitcher Orlin "Buck" Rogers induced a harmless popout to second by Bill Knickerbocker but gave up a single to Roy Hughes. In what was, at the time, the highlight of Rogers' career, he struck out Earl Averill. On that whiff, though, Hughes stole second and moved to third on catcher Chick Starr's throwing error. A Joe Vosmik single drove in Hughes, and an Odell Hale hit pushed Vosmik to third.

Hitting sixth, in part due to the severity of his season-long slump, Trosky stepped into the batter's box. From the right side. Teammates, reporters, and fans were, if not stunned, at least surprised to see the big Bohemian bat as a right-hander. They were even more astonished when he laced a Rogers curve into left field for a base hit and an RBI. Trosky was forced at second by the final batter of the inning, but Cleveland had an early 2–0 lead before Willis Hudlin threw his first pitch.

A long-time Trosky teammate, from 1933–1940, Wagoner, Oklahoma's Willis Hudlin was a lot more than just the pitcher who gave up Babe Ruth's 500th homer. He had a "wicked sidearm sinker"[7] that kept his infield lively, although he was primarily an overhand pitcher, and he won 158 games over a 16-year career with the Indians, Senators, Browns and Giants. After his major league clock expired, and after a stint as a flight instructor during World War II, he went to the minors, to Little Rock, as player-manager, and eventually ended up buying a share of the franchise.[8] He later worked as the pitching coach for the Detroit Tigers from 1957–1959, and finally was a scout for the Yankees before retiring.[9]

Hudlin failed to shut down Washington in the bottom of the inning, giving up a run on John Stone's triple and a Buddy Myer groundout, but held the score at 2–1 through the next frame as well. In the Indians' third, the visitors scored four times, although Trosky—again batting as a righty—could manage only a fly ball to the center fielder. The Indians chased Rogers from his only big league start (and loss) after only two and two-thirds innings.

As a side-note, the individual biographies of even the most obscure ballplayers are often as interesting as those of Hall of Famers. Although Orlin Rogers' major league career lasted all of two games, he would go on to live a wonderfully satisfying life. On the day the Indians stuck a dagger into his baseball dreams, Rogers was barely four months removed from graduation from the University of Virginia. With a degree in economics and prospects for a bright future in hand, he still fell prey to the boy's dream of baseball stardom. When a Senators scout offered him a contract to continue pitching, naturally Rogers signed. After an abbreviated summer as a starter for the Harrisburg Senators (then in the Class A New York-Penn league), where he posted an 11–5 record with a 2.94 ERA, the big Senators summoned him to the capital for a September cup of coffee.

Rogers made one more appearance for Washington that year, tossing seven and one-third innings in relief of Bump Hadley on September 24. He gave up nine runs to the Yankees that afternoon, although he did strike out Lou Gehrig. Remarkably, in his ten big league innings, Rogers struck out seven hitters, two of whom were ultimately bound for Cooperstown. Yet after four more seasons kicking around the minors, followed by a shoulder injury, he finally quit baseball and headed home. In 1943 he was drafted into the Army, saw action in World War II and Korea, and in 1958 joined the faculty at Hargrave Military Academy.[10] He died a happy man in 1999, at the age of 86.

But back in Washington, right-hander Ed Linke relieved Rogers and gave up two unearned runs before finally inducing Hudlin to ground out to second. The Senators answered with a run in their half of the third, and another in the fourth, and Trosky came to bat as a lefty in the fifth. He walked and went to third on right fielder Ab Wright's single, then—in one of the great buried leads in Cleveland sports history—actually stole home (on a double steal) to give the Indians a 7–3 advantage.

By the eighth inning, the visitors enjoyed a 14–4 lead. Trosky led off the inning with a right-handed stance and this time hammered a Leon Pettit pitch into the distant reaches of Griffith Stadium's left field for his 23rd homer of the year.[11] Perhaps the most remarkable aspect of that opposite-side homer was the distance. While there were no tape measurements of home run distances at the time, Griffith's left field foul pole stood 405 feet from home plate. Left field in D.C. was one of those places where long fly balls normally became long fly outs.

In the second game, again batting sixth, Trosky came up in the top of the first, again as a right-hander. With Vosmik and Hale on base, Trosky singled to drive in Vosmik, and in the third inning, again from the right side, he popped out to the catcher in foul territory. He struck out in the fifth.

The seventh inning was a near-replay of the first, as Vosmik and Hale stood on third and first base respectively. Trosky again batted from the right side and again rapped an RBI single to the shortstop. Finally, Trosky returned to his natural stance in the ninth and smoked a double to right field off Jack Russell. He later scored on Wright's single, and the Indians swept the day with a 6–3 victory.[12]

Nine Consecutive Hits— September 13–16, 1936

On September 13, 1936, still two months shy of his 18th birthday and with his senior year of high school still ahead of him, Bob Feller broke Rube Waddell's 28-year-old American League record by striking out 17 Athletics in a single game. It was the first game of a doubleheader with Philadelphia, and the threat of rain in upper Ohio limited the gate to only about 6,000 Indians loyalists. Those fans, however, were treated to an almost inconceivable bit of history as the student blew away his elders. A 17-year-old striking out 17 big league batters, one for each year of the pitcher's life—it was virtually the inverse of older players shooting their age in golf. It is also a mark that will be almost impossible to exceed in the future.

Feller's first baseman that afternoon, Hal Trosky, contributed two singles, along with a ground out and a foul popout to the catcher, in the 5–2 Cleveland win. In the nightcap, behind pitcher Denny Galehouse, Trosky singled in the first inning and doubled in the third before grounding out to lead off the bottom of the sixth. In the seventh inning, with Roy Hughes on third and Earl Averill on first, Trosky homered to drive the winning runs in the Indians' sweep.

After a day off on Monday, Boston arrived in Cleveland for a brief, two-day stopover. On Tuesday, September 15, Trosky was penciled in the cleanup spot and came to bat in the first against young Jennings Poindexter. Almost inevitably, or so it seemed on the blond slugger's bigger days, Brick Owens was again behind the plate in the umpire crouch. Hughes, Knickerbocker, Averill and Trosky all walked, and Trosky notched an RBI even though the plate appearance was not an official at-bat. After a fly out and an Odell Hale RBI single, Poindexter was gone after just one-third of an inning. Reliever Jim Henry fared only a bit better, giving up one more run before finally retiring the home team.

Indians starter Johnny Allen, already with 19 wins on the year, set down the Red Sox in the second and third innings. In the bottom of the third, Trosky led off with a single and scored on Roy Weatherly's triple. In the fourth, Trosky drove in a run with a two-out double, and Allen took the mound in the fifth with a 7–1 lead. With two out and two on due to walks, disaster struck Allen when he pulled a muscle in his back while pitching to his Boston counterpart. After some deliberation, O'Neill pulled the volatile starter. Allen was seeking his 20th win of the year and had yet to give up a hit on the day, but he was simply unable to continue. Oral Hildebrand was summoned from the bullpen and immediately gave up an RBI single to Bill Werber, the first Red Sox hit of the afternoon.

The game moved along uneventfully until the home half of the sixth, when Trosky launched a three-run homer. In the eighth, with the Indians now leading, 10–2, he knocked a two-run bomb off Stew Bowers. By the time Cleveland recorded the final out, a Werber fly ball to left, the score was 13–2.

Interestingly, Johnny Allen earned the win despite not completing five innings as a starter. The scorer's rationale lay in the wording of the applicable rule, that it was not mandatory to withhold the credit from the starter who had not pitched five innings:

> If ... he is taken out because of his team having secured a commanding and winning lead in a few innings, or is forced to retire through injury or illness, or is removed from the game by the umpire when his team has a commanding lead ... the good judgment of the scorer must determine in such cases, as much depends on whether the pitcher was relieved because of ineffectiveness or for other reasons.

That decision might have enjoyed a bit more scrutiny, along with a few angry emails, in later times, but held up without much comment in 1936.

Lost in all that was Trosky's 4-for-4 day at the plate, with two home runs, seven RBI, and 11 total bases. The game took only two hours and 16 minutes and was played in front of fewer than 1,000 spectators,[13] but he had hit safely in five straight at-bats, and also became the first Cleveland Indian to hit 40 home runs in a single season.

The following afternoon, September 16, again found Trosky in the fourth spot in the lineup. With weather again an issue, and neither team playing particularly well, only 500 fans showed up to watch Boston's Ted Olson, an Ivy Leaguer from Dartmouth, take on Iowa's young Bill Zuber, making his big league debut.

Although Zuber's life has been chronicled in an excellent book, *Now Pitching From Amana: Bill Zuber*, his story is one of those that could only spring from a place like eastern Iowa. He was born and raised in the Amana Colonies of Iowa, a self-sufficient German commune that, until the "great change" in 1932, was virtually cut off from the rest of society. Zuber required permission of the Amana Society just to be allowed to play industrial league baseball in Cedar Rapids after Cy Slapnicka had discovered him.

Bill Zuber was gifted, certainly good enough to pitch nearly 800 innings in the major leagues—and finished with a career winning record—before retiring to his restaurant in 1947.

The September 16 Cleveland-Boston game was delayed 20 minutes due to rain, a drizzle that never abated that day, and Zuber had a relatively easy first inning. After Hughes grounded out to open the bottom half and Bill Knickerbocker walked, Vosmik flied to center for the second out. Trosky then homered for his sixth straight hit. By the time Zuber took the mound again, he enjoyed a 4–0 lead.

146

In the Indians' second, Trosky singled and scored on Odell Hale's triple to right field. In the fourth, with Cleveland up, 8–1, he doubled to right and immediately scored on Bruce Campbell's follow-up double. In the fifth, with two outs and two on, he singled to center for his ninth consecutive hit. He scored again on a Campbell hit, and at the end of the inning the score stood at 13–3 in favor of the home team. The Red Sox failed to score in the sixth, and the game was halted for a bit as the rainfall approached torrential. Umpire Lou Kolls finally called it after the Indians were retired in the sixth, evidently deciding that a 13–3 lead was enough to justify an early stop.[14]

Even though the game ended prematurely, Trosky found himself sitting on nine hits in nine at-bats, only two behind Tris Speaker's 1920 major league record. The next day his bid for the record didn't last past the second inning. Facing Detroit's Jake Wade, he "swung viciously at one of Wade's fastballs…. The ball caromed off his bat and struck him on the ankle. Trosky dropped to the ground and was unable to rise for several minutes. He rolled weakly to Charlie Gehringer to snap his sensational hitting streak and then retired from the game."[15] The streak was over. Trosky wouldn't play again until the following Tuesday.

Playing for the Pennant—September 27, 1940

For the Friday game 45,553 fans passed through the turnstyles at Cleveland Stadium. The Tigers lineup not only included Gehringer and Greenberg, but also slugging outfielder Rudy York and former Indians Bruce Campbell and catcher Billy Sullivan in support of young Floyd Giebell. Bill Summers was the chief umpire, and oversaw a full crew of Harry Geisel, Steve Basil, and George Pipgras. The top of the first inning passed quickly. Feller walked Dick Bartell, but a 4–6–3 double play and a Gehringer fly out ended the frame without further incident.

In the bottom of the first inning, the crowd deluged Hank Greenberg, now in left field to make room for York's hat at first base, with all sorts of spoiled produce. The umpire called time and warned the crowd that he would pull the entire Detroit squad off the field if the rowdiness continued. Ben Chapman led off the Indians' effort with a walk, but Giebell also induced a fly out and a double-play grounder to set the home team down without a threat.

The second inning was marred when a fan dumped some bottles over the railing in the upper deck. One of the bottles knocked Birdie Tebbetts out cold, prompting Oscar Vitt to take the microphone and beg the crowd to stop. The aerial assault abated and the game continued in a scoreless tie despite a Greenberg double.

In the third inning, Feller settled into his rhythm. He struck out two batters and eliminated Giebell on a weak grounder to first. In the bottom of the inning, second baseman Ray Mack reached first on an error. Rollie Hemsley singled to push Mack to third base, but Giebell rose to the moment and struck out both Feller and Ben Chapman. The top of the fourth was Detroit's moment to challenge. With one out, Feller walked Charlie Gehringer but fanned the fearsome Greenberg. The situation was seemingly under control, with a man on first and two down, when Rudy York lifted a soft fly ball to left field. The ball hung in the sky, drifting gently, until Ben Chapman stretched out his glove for a long third out.

Except that Chapman didn't catch the ball.

It bounced off his glove and over the fence for a home run at the left field foul pole, staking Detroit to a 2–0 lead. That Feller would give up only two more hits all afternoon was immaterial; the damage had been done.

The Indians had their chances. In the bottom of the fourth, Beau Bell and Ken Keltner both singled with two outs, but Ray Mack struck out to end the threat. In the fifth, Rollie Hemsley singled and Feller walked. But two strikeouts and one harmless Roy Weatherly flyout later, the inning was over. In the bottom of the seventh, Mack singled up the middle and Hemsley again reached first—this time on a rare Gehringer error—to put runners at first and second. Feller sacrificed the runners to second and third, but Giebell fanned Chapman for the third time and retired Weatherly to kill the threat.

The eighth and ninth innings were a quiet formality before the Indians officially conceded game, season, and pennant to the Tigers. That night, Philadelphia beat the Yankees to mathematically seal the 1940 American League season for Detroit. Cleveland won the final two games of the year against the champion Tigers, so the official standings show a one-game margin, but the season ended that Friday afternoon. Baker's gambit with Giebell worked so well that it seemed scripted.

Trosky's Final Game—September 27, 1946

The final Friday of Chicago's season found the White Sox hosting the St. Louis Browns at Comiskey Park. Given the positional poverty of both teams—neither could end with a winning record—only 3,609 fans showed for the doubleheader. The Sox won the opener, 7–3, getting a complete game from Eddie Lopat, and sent Frank Papish to the mound to face the Browns' ace (okay, the only starter on the roster with a winning record), Jack Kramer, in the nightcap. Trosky batted third in the order, behind Thurman Tucker and Luke Appling, and started at first base.

Papish gave up a leadoff single to rookie infielder Bob Dillinger in the top of the first, then picked him off to reset the bases. After he retired Al Zarilla and Paul Lehner, the White Sox came to bat.

A Tucker single and a Trosky walk, followed by a Kramer balk, put runners on second and third with only one out. Taft Wright hit a grounder to score Tucker, but was ejected by Art Passarella for arguing the call at first. Dave Philley tripled to drive in Trosky, and by the time the Sox were retired, they enjoyed a 3–0 lead.

With the exception of one Browns single, the second inning was an uneventful six-up-six-down frame. In the bottom of the third, seemingly aware that his baseball career was soon to end, Trosky tripled off Kramer and promptly scored when Bob Kennedy hit a three-bagger of his own. The score remained 5–0 through the fifth, but St. Louis scored three runs in the sixth and Chicago managed only one run as a response.

Trosky led off the bottom of the seventh with an out, but Chicago scored twice to raise the lead to 8–3. The Browns went silently in the eighth. The Sox opened their eighth with a Tucker out and a Luke Appling single. With one out and one on, Trosky came to bat for what would be the final time of his career, and with an opportunity to drive in one more run for the books. Baseball, however, can be occasionally ruthless and cruel. Trosky, fittingly, pulled a ground ball to second baseman Johnny Berardino, who flipped it to shortstop Vern Stephens to force Appling, and then on to first baseman Chuck Stevens for the double play.[16]

Chicago set down the Browns in order in the ninth for an 8–3 final score and a doubleheader sweep. The final swing notwithstanding,

Trosky had one of his best days with the White Sox, with a triple, a walk, and two runs scored in a win. The game was a fitting finale for the big man. Joe Kuhel played first base for Chicago in the season-ender on Sunday—going 2-for-5 in an 8–7 loss—and Trosky's season was over. One more interesting point about Trosky: hitting a triple in his final game exactly replicated the final hit of Billy Hoffer, an earlier star player from Cedar Rapids who also played for the Indians in his closing appearance back in 1901. The circle finally closed.

Career Statistics

Figures in **bold** represent Trosky's personal career highs.

Year	Age	G	R	H	2B	HR	RBI	BA	SLG	OPS	TB
1933	20	11	6	13	1	1	8	.295	.477	.818	21
1934	21	**154**	117	206	**45**	35	142	.330	.598	.987	374
1935	22	**154**	84	171	33	26	113	.271	.468	.789	296
1936	23	151	**124**	**216**	**45**	**42**	**162**	**.343**	**.644**	**1.026**	**405**
1937	24	153	104	179	36	32	128	.298	.547	.915	329
1938	25	150	106	185	40	19	110	.334	.542	.948	300
1939	26	122	89	150	31	25	104	.335	.589	.994	264
1940	27	140	85	154	39	25	93	.295	.529	.920	276
1941	28	89	43	91	17	11	51	.294	.455	.838	141
1944	31	135	55	120	32	10	70	.241	.374	.701	186
1946	33	88	22	76	12	2	31	.254	.334	.665	100
Total		1347	835	1561	331	228	1012	.302	.522	.892	2692
Cleveland		1124	758	1365	287	216	911	.313	.551	.930	2406
Chicago		223	77	196	44	12	101	.246	.359	.687	286
162 Game Avg.			100	188	40	27	122	.302	.522	.892	324

A Note on Sources

Any attempt to tell the life story of a baseball player who last played seven decades ago, and who passed away more than 35 years ago, is laden with embedded challenges. Especially daunting is the scarcity of first-person eyewitnesses to the events described. Within this biography, every quotation was either taken directly from a personal interview or copied verbatim from a published, primary source. The problems stemming from this approach, from a historian's perspective, are two-fold. One evil is that many of those sources were/are clippings without attribution. The availability of the personal scrapbooks of Lorraine Trosky, Susan Volz, KC Waychoff, Steve Benedict, and Harold "Pinky" Primrose, along with Hal Trosky's clippings file at the Giamatti Research Center in the National Baseball Hall of Fame in Cooperstown (provided by Tim Wiles and Freddy Berowski) offered me access to a gamut of newspaper articles and documents otherwise lost to history (and the eastern Iowa flood of 2008). Unfortunately, the demise of so many of the other newspapers and accounts of the time may create unintentional, imbalanced bias in recounting Trosky's life.

Along with those sources, much of what remains regarding Trosky's life and career has been archived by the indefatigable Shona Frese, the director of the Iowa Baseball Museum of Norway. Her clipping files are the most complete anywhere and are available to any researcher wishing to continue down this road. The terrific team at the Benton County Historical Society in Vinton, Iowa, provided me with a special Bing Miller archive, and are a great repository of knowledge about not only the Miller family but about rural Iowa and Benton County a century ago. The researchers at both the State Historical Society of Iowa and the Cedar Rapids Historical Society were also quite

152

gracious in helping me learn about eastern Iowa before 1920. Many of those clippings, as described earlier, however, did not come with source and author bylines.

When discussing sources for any Iowa baseball research project, Professor John Liepa, of Indianola, is both the first and last word on the topic. He has forgotten more about Iowa's baseball history than most of us may ever discover, and is the primary source on the origins and spread of the game throughout the state and the Midwest. His research files, alone, saved hundreds of hours of searching through archives and microfilm.

Russell Schneider, in addition to curating the best museum-in-print of the Cleveland Indians (*Cleveland Indians Encyclopedia*; Champaign: Sports Publishing, 2001), was encouraging early on and helped me connect with both the Indians and White Sox. The representatives of both of those organizations were invaluable in helping me locate then-living former teammates of Hal Trosky.

I have been fortunate to interview several former major league baseball players about Trosky. One of the unanticipated advantages of starting this project in the early 1990s is that I was able to speak, or exchange letters, with men who are no longer with us. That list includes, in no particular order, Bob Feller, Mel Harder, Rick Ferrell, Willis Hudlin, Elden Auker, Denny Galehouse, Roy Hughes, Thornton Lee, Ralph Hodgin, and—of course—Hal's eldest son Hal Trosky, Jr. Each of those men was gracious and forthcoming in sharing particular memories of their time with Hal, even if those memories were becoming attenuated over time.

Regarding the history of baseball in Cedar Rapids, Bruce Kimm and Mike Boddicker are two of the great gentlemen from Iowa who also had notable baseball gifts, and were easy to interview. Similarly, Cedar Rapids Kernels historian Marcia Moran arranged opportunities for me to meet and talk with former 1961 Cedar Rapids Braves Barry Morgan and Ron Hunt. Hunt, a 1964 National League All-Star with the New York Mets, can be refreshingly blunt, but both of those men (and Mrs. Hunt) were beyond cordial in sharing their private memories with a complete stranger. One of the challenges inherent in talking to some former players, especially those from Iowa, is that their collective veneer of humility is core-deep and completely genuine. Not only are they generally reticent in talking about themselves and their respective careers, but they are much more comfortable talking about their old teammates and their old teams.

Two player wives were also extraordinarily patient. Lorraine Trosky, in many ways, made this entire work possible by opening her home and her memory to me back in 1997. Along with Bill Zuber's widow, Connie, I've been afforded a peek behind the curtain, a glimpse of the life of a major league baseball family back in the 1930s and 1940s. Hal's son, Jim, and Bill's daughter, Connie Baugh, were also wonderful in sharing specific memories of their respective fathers and provided a perspective often ignored in this genre of sports history.

Then there are the books and magazine articles that buttressed this effort. Raymond Sweeney's master's thesis for MIT, *The American Ballpark: A Structural Perspective*, contains a wonderfully succinct introduction to the jewel-box ballparks of the early twentieth century. Franklin "Whitey" Lewis' 1949 opus *The Cleveland Indians* is the most complete team history written before 1950, and his thoughts on Trosky's years with the team were still relatively fresh when Lewis penned his book. Professor George Wiley, in 1990, wrote the now out-of-print monograph on the 1936 Cleveland Indians and their 357 doubles (31 more than Detroit), and effectively argued that while the odd configuration of League Park conferred some advantage to the left-handed sluggers on that squad, the park was not as much a contributor as some revisionists have posited.

Other secondary source material included a March 1879 article in *Scribner's Monthly* by Edward Eggleston entitled "Some Western School-Masters," and an unpublished 2010 dissertation by Hugh Mac-Dowell cited by Brian Martin in his amazing book *Baseball's Creation Myth*, "Abner Graves: The Man Who Brought Baseball to Cooperstown," is a great source of information about that particular slice of baseball's history.

In addition to interviewing Elden Auker in 1995, his book *Sleeping Cars and Flannel Uniforms* (Chicago: Triumph Books, 2006) is a gem and I recommend it highly, along with Cliff Trumpold's *Now Pitching From Amana: Bill Zuber*. Similarly, the *Minor League Encyclopedia* (third edition), edited by Miles Wolff and W. Lloyd Johnson and published by *Baseball America*, contains a wealth of verified background information that I was unable to find elsewhere.

Finally, in terms of other periodicals, various *Life* magazines from the 1930s have nuggets of useful history, as does *American Heritage*. In the latter, specifically, a May 1970 article titled "How to Score From First on a Sacrifice" (available online at www.americanheritage.com/articles/magazine/ah/1970/5/1970_5_30.shtml) by James "Cool Papa" Bell and seminal Negro leagues historian John Holway is fascinating, as is Bill Dow's August 2009 *Baseball Digest* article, "Mark Fidrych's Personal Catcher, Bruce Kimm, Remembers 'The Bird.'" And I while I did not discover this particular article until very late in the process, Jim Odenkirk's "Not Tolstoy, Not Trotsky, but Harold 'Hal' Trosky: The Rise and Fall of Hal Trosky," originally published in the Fall 2002 edition of *Nine: A Journal of Baseball History and Culture*, along with Ira Smith's 1956 book *Baseball's Famous First Basemen*, for a long time was the only published summary of Trosky's life. Odenkirk is an expert on the Cleveland Indians and I recommend any of his pieces to all Tribe fans.

This leaves the interviews and conversations, of which there have been many. In addition to the above summary, I have gathered detail, connections, and perspective from the following people: Richard "Butch" Boddicker, Bob Lana, Bill Quinby, Bob Meyer, Rick Ryan, Steve Stumpff, Dorothy Voutrebek, Fred Schuld, Susan Volz, Pinky and Flo Primrose, Gayle Holt, and the entire family of Ray Waychoff, including KC, Kathy, Joanne, and Blaine, who gave me a look at Trosky's times. Similar conversations with Rick Ryan, Bernie Hutchison, Jim Van Scoyoc, and Nick Zumsande each helped me flesh out the Norway-Cedar Rapids baseball connection and the meaning of Trosky's success in shaping the baseball ethos of the region.

In terms of statistics, every number cited herein comes from Baseball-Reference.com. Game summaries were culled from either the relevant newspaper of the day or from the marvelous website Retrosheet.com. In terms of additional online research, there are some amazing baseball websites. The Society of American Baseball Research (SABR) hosts what is, I believe, the single best repository of links and research for any baseball-related topic—had this existed 20 years ago, I might have had the wherewithal to complete this project years earlier. Anyone embarking on a similar journey should start with SABR and move forward from there. In addition, the SABR (Iowa) "Field of Dreams" Chapter hosts a web-based repository on Iowa's baseball history, and SABR's *Baseball Research Journal*—around since 1971—is a font of otherwise unavailable research.

A Note on Sources

An array of other sources captures the history of the city of Cleveland as well, including the web repository of the Cleveland Historical Society and an "Encyclopedia of Cleveland History," a joint project of Case Western Reserve University and the Western Reserve Historical Society (online: http://ech.cwru.edu/). For an engaging snapshot of the tail end of Cleveland's golden age, the book *Full Face*, published by the Gruber Hollenden Foundation of Cleveland in 1954, and edited by sportswriters Ed Bang, Gordon Cobbledick, and Franklin Lewis, is a fascinating glimpse back in time.

In terms of photos, Cassidy Lent and John Horne of the National Baseball Hall of Fame, and Donna Stewart and Lynn Duchez Bycko of Cleveland State University, provided some of the wonderful photos in the book.

Finally, while not technically source-related, the editorial and technical mentorship and oversight from Chuck Hilty, Jan Finkel, J. R. Ogden, and Mark Dukes is impossible to quantify. Without them this would not have been possible.

Chapter Notes

Chapter 1

1. Every quotation attributed to Hal Trosky herein was taken verbatim from a newspaper or magazine of the day. Many of these articles were clipped and pasted into scrapbooks, which is fortunate because many of those sources no longer exist. As newspapers and periodicals consolidated over time, the digitization and cataloging of their contents has often been neglected. There are no dates for articles from Susan Volz's scrapbook.
2. Archived materials from the Benton County Historical Society in Vinton, Iowa.
3. Jeff Holmes, "Bing Miller—A Star in an Era of Superstars," *Cedar Valley Times*, August 15, 1990.
4. *Ibid.*
5. Terry Turner, "Arkansas Travelers," Encyclopedia of Arkansas History and Culture (website), http://www.encyclopediaofarkansas.net/encyclopedia/entry-detail.aspx?entryID=1180.
6. Bill Johnson, "Bing Miller," Society for American Baseball Research (SABR) BioProject, online: http://sabr.org/bioproj/person/e6ec9e64.
7. *The Sporting News*, March 14, 1935, 4.
8. *The Sporting News*, June 28, 1934, 4.
9. Gordon Cobbledick, *Cleveland Plain Dealer*, 1935. Clipping from the archives of the National Baseball Hall of Fame, Cooperstown, New York.
10. Interview with Hal Trosky, Jr., October 12, 2012.

11. Correspondence with Denny Galehouse and Thornton Lee, 1994.
12. Kevin Kerrane, *Dollar Sign on the Muscle* (New York: Beaufort Books, 1984), 30–31.
13. Tait Cummins, *Cedar Rapids Gazette*. Clipping from the scrapbook of Susan Volz.
14. Leslie Heaphy, ed., *Black Baseball in Chicago* (Jefferson, NC: McFarland, 2006).
15. Lawrence D. Hogan, ed., *Shades of Glory: The Negro Leagues and the Story of African American Baseball* (Washington, DC: National Geographic, 2006), 91–92.
16. *Ibid.*
17. *Muscatine (IA) Journal*, May 8, 1931.
18. *Ibid.*
19. Interview with Harold Primrose, 2009.
20. "Art Pennington," Negro League Baseball Museum, College of Education, Kansas State University, http://coe.k-state.edu/annex/nlbmuseum/history/players/pennington.html.
21. Gordon Cobbledick, *Cleveland Plain Dealer*, from the scrapbook of Susan Volz.
22. *The Sporting News*, June 28, 1934, 4.
23. Dick Meade, *Toledo News-Bee*, 1933, from scrapbook of Susan Volz.

Chapter 2

1. Heidi Fearing, "John D. Rockefeller," Cleveland Historical Society web-

site, http://clevelandhistorical.org/items/show/328#.Vrn_JtDPjfY.

2. *Encyclopedia of Cleveland History*, online: http://ech.case.edu/cgi/article.pl?id=I4.

3. Interview with Willis Hudlin, June 1994.

4. Tait Cummins article, from the scrapbook of Susan Volz.

5. *Ibid.*

Chapter 3

1. Clipping from the scrapbook of Susan Volz.

2. *The Sporting News*, March 15, 1934.

3. Gordon Cobbledick "Advice Trosky Gets Like Man Biting Dog" *Cleveland Plain Dealer*, April 6, 1935, 19.

4. *The Sporting News*, January 11, 1934, 2.

5. *The Sporting News*, February 9, 1934, 3.

6. Cobbledick, "Advice Trosky Gets Like Man Biting Dog," *Cleveland Plain Dealer*, April 6, 1935.

7. *Ibid.*

8. John Tattersall "Clarifying an Early Home Run Record," *Baseball Research Journal* vol. 1(1972), http://sabr.org/research/clarifying-early-home-run-record.

9. *Ibid.*

10. Dan Daniel, "Hal Trosky, Prize Rookie of the Year," *New York World-Telegram*, undated, from scrapbook of Susan Volz.

11. Dan Daniel, in a clipping from scrapbook of Susan Volz.

Chapter 4

1. Interview with Elden Auker, January 1995.

2. *The Sporting News*, February 10, 1935, 3B.

3. *Ibid.*

4. Ed Bang "O'Neill, Sticking as Manager, Seeks Catcher to Boost Tribe," *The Sporting News*, September 26, 1935, 3.

5. *The Sporting News*, March 13, 1935, 1.

6. *The Sporting News*, April 18, 1935, 2.

7. Russell Schneider, *The Cleveland Indians Encyclopedia*, 3d ed. (Champaign, IL: Sports Publishing, 2005), 328.

8. Franklin Lewis, *The Cleveland Indians*, 1949.

9. Schneider, 327.

10. *Ibid.*

11. Ed Bang, "Lo, The Poor Indians, They Scalp Selves," *The Sporting News*, July 11, 1935, 5.

12. Ed Bang, "Hal Trosky Leaves No Room for Foxx," *The Sporting News*, October 24, 1935.

13. Clipping from Susan Volz collection. This is partially corroborated in the August 5, 1935, *Chicago Tribune* (online: http://archives.chicagotribune.com/1935/08/05/page/15/article/comic-2-no-title).

14. Ed Bang, *Cleveland News*, July 17, 1934; quoted in Schneider, *The Cleveland Indians Encyclopedia*, 3d ed., 253.

15. Gary Sarnoff *The Wrecking Crew of '33: The Washington Senators' Last Pennant* (Jefferson, NC: McFarland, 2009), 6.

16. Lewis, *Cleveland Indians*. Chapter 18 (page unknown—hold Kindle version).

17. Obituary of Alva Bradley *New York Times*, March 30, 1953.

18. Ed Bang, *The Sporting News*, September 26, 1935.

19. *Cleveland Plain Dealer*, August 21, 1935, 19.

20. "Switch Shakes Trosky's Slump," Clipping from unidentified news article in archives of Norway Baseball Museum, Norway, IA.

21. "Trosky Gives Bat Switch Longer Trial," undated article from the Norway Baseball Museum, Norway, IA.

22. *Ibid.*

23. Ed Bang, *The Sporting News*, October 24, 1935.

24. Interview of Rick Ferrell, June 1994.

25. Ed Bang, *The Sporting News*, October 24, 1935.

26. *Ibid.*

27. "Billy Evans, Renowned Baseball Figure, Dies," *Youngstown Vindicator*, January 24, 1956.

Chapter 5

1. Interview with Willis Hudlin, July 1994.

2. Baseball-Reference.com, http://www.baseball-reference.com/players/t/troskha01.shtml.

3. Clipping from scrapbook of Susan Volz.

4. Ed Bang, "O'Neill Stands Pat on Hale for Third," *The Sporting News*, January 30, 1936.

5. Gordon Cobbledick, "Opener Lost, Tribe's Going Places Now, Undaunted Fans Say," *Cleveland Plain Dealer*, April 15, 1936.

6. Clipping from the scrapbook of Susan Volz.

7. Gordon Cobbledick, "Campbell Fights for Life Again," *Cleveland Plain Dealer*, May 2, 1936.

8. Clipping from the scrapbook of Susan Volz.

9. Ed Bang, "Tribe Fans 'Fed Up' on Feast of Alibis," *The Sporting News*, June 25, 1936.

10. Ed McAuley, "Weatherly Clears Cleveland Sky of Clouds," *The Sporting News*, August 6, 1936.

11. David Pietrusza, Matthew Silverman, Michael Gershman, and Mikhail Horowitz, "The Top 100 Players," *Total Baseball*, 7th ed. (Kingston, NY: Total Sports Publishing, 2001), 126.

12. Ferrell interview, 1994.

13. Clipping from the scrapbook of Susan Volz.

14. Telephone interview with Bob Feller, November 1994.

15. *Cleveland Indians Media Guide*, 2011.

16. Interview with Feller, 1994.

17. Ed Bang, "Bob Feller Contract Lesson Starts Tribe Back-to-the-Farm Movement," *The Sporting News*, December 31, 1936.

18. Ed Bang, "Tribal Changes Indicate Hale May Return to Post at Second," *The Sporting News*, October 8, 1936.

19. Ed Bang, "Vosmik In Big Deal Signs Up With Cupid," *The Sporting News*, November 5, 1936, 5.

20. Baseball-Reference.com, www.baseball-reference.com.

21. George Wiley, "One Wall and 357 Doubles: The Story of the 1936 Cleveland Indians," presentation to the Society for American Baseball Research, Cleveland, OH, July 1990.

22. *Ibid.*

Chapter 6

1. Letter from Mel Harder to author, December 1996.

2. Interview with Hal Trosky, Jr., 2012.

3. Elden Auker, *Sleeping Cars and Flannel Uniforms: A Lifetime of Memories From Striking Out the Babe to Teeing it Up With the President* (Chicago: Triumph Books, 2006). Page 95

4. Ed McAuley, "Fans Shout 'We Want Feller' At Every Stop On Tribe Tour," *The Sporting News*, April 15, 1937.

5. Ed Bang, "Best Staff in A.L. Just a Tribe Worry," *The Sporting News*, May 6, 1937.

6. Ed Bang, "Tribal Chief Goes on Warpath, Bars Poker, Orders Early Rising," *The Sporting News*, June 24, 1937.

7. *Ibid.*

8. Box score from Retrosheet, http://www.retrosheet.org/boxesetc/1937/B07051SLA1937.htm.

9. "Back in Hit Parade," *The Sporting News*, July 22, 1937.

10. Ed Bang, "Indians Under Vitt to Need Moccasins," *The Sporting News*, November 4, 1937.

11. "Trailblazers for Tribe: Chiefs of Cleveland," *The Sporting News*, December 2, 1937.

12. Van Craddock, "The Judge Ruled 'Foul' in Diamond Dispute," *Longview News-Journal*, July 31, 2010, http://www.news-journal.com/news/2010/jul/31/craddock-the-judge-ruled-foul-in-diamond-dispute.

13. "Managers and Umps Tell It to Judge Today," *Cleveland Plain Dealer*, April 16, 1938.

14. Gordon Cobbledick, "Hal's 3 Hits to Left Elevate Vitt," *Cleveland Plain Dealer*, March 17, 1938, 16.

15. Tom Verducci, "As shifts suppress offense, time has come to consider a rule change," *Sports Illustrated*, July 22, 2014, http://www.si.com/mlb/2014/07/22/shifts-rule-change-lefthanded-batters-david-ortiz.

16. Gordon Cobbledick, "Hal's 3 Hits to Left Elevate Vitt," March 17, 1938.

17. "Vitt Trying To Pull 'Pull' Out of Trosky," *The Sporting News*, March 24, 1938.

18. Quoted in Jack De Vries, "Cleveland's Great Achilles: Hal Trosky," *Gameface*, May 25, 1998, http://www.indians.com/gameface/feature/trosky.html.

19. Gordon Cobbledick, "Hal's 3 Hits to Left Elevate Vitt," March 17, 1938.

20. Clipping from the scrapbook of Susan Volz.

21. *Ibid.*

22. *Ibid.*

23. "Snubbing of Trosky by M'Carthy Stirs Up All-Star Storm in A.L.," *The Sporting News*, July 7, 1938.

24. "Trosky Glad Americans Lost All-Star Contest," *New York Times*, July 8, 1938.

25. Gordon Cobbledick, "Hal Did Nothing to Earn Increase, Bradley Asserts," *Cleveland Plain Dealer*, February 14, 1939, 14.

26. Interview with Hal Trosky, Jr., October 2012.

27. Clipping from the scrapbook of Lorraine Trosky, 1996.

28. Ed McAuley, "Explosive Bat Booms Trosky Back in Hearts of Tribe Fans," *The Sporting News*, September 7, 1939, 3.

29. "Introducing Hal Trosky," *Cleveland Plain Dealer*, July 15, 1939; "Hal 'Trosky' Isn't Trojovsky Any More," *The Sporting News*, July 14, 1939.

30. Interview with Lorraine Trosky, August 1996.

Chapter 7

1. Frederick G. Lieb, "Nationals Upset of A.L. Stars Home-Town Triumph for Lopez," *The Sporting News*, March 21, 1940, 2.

2. "Trosky's Son Perks Up as Hal Gets to Hospital," *Cleveland Plain Dealer*, May 2, 1940.

3. *Ibid.*

4. Bob Dolgan, "Vitt's 'Cry Babies' Revolt of 20 Years Ago Recalled," *Cleveland Plain Dealer*, June 12, 1960, 7-C.

5. Clipping from the scrapbook of Susan Volz.

6. Robert Creamer, *Baseball in '41* (New York: Viking, 1991), 161.

7. Cliff Trumpold, *Now Pitching: Bill Zuber From Amana* (Amana, IA: Lakeview Press, 1992), page 72.

8. De Vries, "Cleveland's Great Achilles: Hal Trosky," *Gameface*, May 25, 1998.

9. Clipping, archives of Norway Baseball Museum.

10. *Ibid.*

11. Hal Lebowitz, "Ask Hal" *Cleveland Plain Dealer*, June January 14, 1979, 2–3.

12. Gordon Cobbledick, "Plain Dealing," *Cleveland Plain Dealer*, June 14, 1940.

13. Untitled article from *Cedar Rapids Gazette*, from scrapbook of Susan Volz.

14. *Ibid.*

15. Maury White, untitled and undated clipping from the *Des Moines Register*, archives of the Norway Baseball Museum.

16. *Ibid.*

17. De Vries, "Cleveland's Great Achilles: Hal Trosky," *Gameface*, May 25, 1998.

18. *Ibid.* Also recounted in conversation with Hal Trosky, Jr.

19. Cited by Russell Schnieder, *Cleveland Indians Encyclopedia*, 3rd ed., 358.

20. *Ibid.*

21. Lebowitz, *Cleveland Plain Dealer*, June 14, 1979, 2–3.

22. Gordon Cobbledick, "Plain Dealing," *Cleveland Plain Dealer*, August 22, 1940.

23. Eugene Whitney, precise source unknown; copied from Trosky file at National Baseball Hall of Fame.

Chapter 8

1. Franklin Lewis, "Trosky is a Chump," *Cleveland Press*, April 1943 (exact date unknown; scrapbook clipping).
2. Ed McAuley, "'Shaken-Up' Tribe Likely to Line-Up Just About Same," *The Sporting News*, February 6, 1941.
3. "Major League Notes," *The Sporting News*, March 6, 1941, 10.
4. Ed McAuley, "Pains in Head Force Trosky to Lay Off," *The Sporting News*, July 17, 1941.
5. *Ibid.*
6. Ed McAuley, "Tribe Gets Earful at Called Meeting," *The Sporting News*, July 3, 1941, 6.
7. De Vries, "Cleveland's Great Achilles: Hal Trosky," *Gameface*, May 25, 1998.
8. Gayle Hayes, "Hal Trosky Quits Baseball," *Des Moines Register*, February 18, 1942.
9. Tait Cummins, "Hal Trosky, Former Star Cleveland First Baseman, Also Stars on Farm," *Cedar Rapids Gazette*, November 8, 1942.
10. Gordon Cobbledick, "Plain Dealing," *Cleveland Plain Dealer*, December 7, 1942.
11. Dan Daniel, "Newcomer Etten Faces Competition for Job," *New York Times*, January 24, 1943.
12. Interview with Lorraine Trosky, 1998.

Chapter 9

1. Tim Bannon, "Sports Flashback: White Sox and Cubs Spring Trainings in French Lick," *Chicago Tribune*, February 20, 2015, http://baseball.com/sports/baseball/cubs/chi-spring-training-in-french-lick-photos-20150220-photogallery.html.
2. *Chicago Tribune*, March 20, 1943.

3. Untitled article from the scrapbook of Susan Volz.
4. Interview with Ralph Hodgin, September 1994.
5. Milt Woodard, "Hal Trosky to Rejoin White Sox Next Year," *Chicago Sun-Times*, 1945. Precise date unknown; article from the archives of the Norway Baseball Museum.
6. *Ibid.*
7. Milt Woodard, "Hal Trosky to Rejoin White Sox Next Year," *Chicago Sun-Times*, 1945.
8. "White Sox Sign Trosky As a Scout," *Cleveland Plain Dealer*, February 12, 1947, 17.
9. Steve Smith, "Emlen Tunnell: A Minor League Less-Than," 2010; online as part of SABR's Field of Dreams (Iowa) chapter's Iowa Baseball Project, http://chapters.sabr.org/fieldofdreams/iowa-baseball-project.
10. Dennis Listing, "Whatever Happened to Hal Trosky?" *Cleveland Plain Dealer*, March 12, 1970, 6-F.
11. Interview and email exchange with James Trosky, July 2015.
12. Interview with Hal Trosky, Jr., 2012.
13. Norman Macht, "The 1.000 Hitter and the Undefeated Pitcher," *Baseball Research Journal* 10 (1989).

Appendix

1. Tait Cummins, untitled and undated article from the *Cedar Rapids Gazette*, from the scrapbook of Susan Volz.
2. Gordon Cobbledick, "Ruth's Two Homers Beat Tribe Twice," *Cleveland Plain Dealer*, September 18, 1933.
3. Box score from Retrosheet.org, http://www.retrosheet.org/boxesetc/1934/B05302CLE1934.htm.
4. Gordon Cobbledick "Trosky's Three Straight Homers Beat White Sox," *Cleveland Plain Dealer*, May 31, 1934, 13.
5. *Ibid.*
6. "Trosky Gives Bat Switch Longer Trial," Clipping from unidentified news article in archives of Norway Baseball Museum.

7. Gordon Cobbledick, "Plain Dealing," *Cleveland Plain Dealer*, August 29, 1944, 14.

8. *Ibid.*

9. Richard Goldstein, "Willis Hudlin, 96, a Pitcher Who Excelled For the Indians," *New York Times*, August 17, 2002.

10. Fred Anderson "Orlin Woodrow Rogers—Still a Country Boy," *Religious Herald, Virginia Baptist Weekly*, November 5, 1998, https://www.geni.com/discussions/147089.

11. Box score from Retrosheet.org, http://www.retrosheet.org/boxesetc/1935/B09151WS11935.htm.

12. Box score from Retrosheet.org, http://www.retrosheet.org/boxesetc/1935/B09152WS11935.htm.

13. Box score from Retrosheet.org, http://www.retrosheet.org/boxesetc/1936/B09150CLE1936.htm.

14. Alex Zirin, "Hal Trosky Belts Nine Hits In A Row," *Cleveland Plain Dealer*, September 17, 1936.

15. "Trosky Hurt, Swat Streak Ends at Nine," *Cleveland Plain Dealer*, September 17, 1936.

16. Box score from Retrosheet.org, http://www.retrosheet.org/boxesetc/1946/B09272CHA1946.htm.

Bibliography

Books and Articles

Alexander, Charles. *Breaking the Slump: Baseball in the Depression Era.* New York: Columbia University Press, 2002.

_____. *John McGraw.* Lincoln: University of Nebraska Press, 1988.

Auker, Eldon, with Tom Keegan. *Sleeper Cars and Flannel Uniforms.* Chicago: Triumph, 2001.

Boudreau, Lou, with Russell Schneider. *Lou Boudreau—Covering All the Bases.* Urbana, IL: Sagamore, 1993.

Clark, Jerry. *Anson to Zuber: Iowa Boys in the Major Leagues.* Omaha: Making History, 1992.

Creamer, Robert. *Baseball in '41.* New York: Viking, 1991.

Doxsie, Don. *Iowa Baseball Greats: Sixteen Major Leaguers Who Were in the Game for Life.* Jefferson, NC: McFarland, 2015.

Feller, Bob, with Bill Gilbert. *Now Pitching Bob Feller.* New York: HarperCollins, 1990.

Heaphy, Leslie, ed. *Black Baseball in Chicago.* Jefferson, NC: McFarland, 2006.

Hogan, Lawrence D., ed. *Shades of Glory: The Negro Leagues and the Story of African American Baseball.* Washington, DC: National Geographic, 2006.

Honig, Donald. *Baseball When the Grass Was Real.* Lincoln: University of Nebraska Press, 1975.

James, Bill. *The New Bill James Historical Abstract.* New York: Simon & Schuster, 2010.

Johnson, William H., and Shona Frese. *Norway Baseball: Gone but Not Forgotten.* Norway, IA: Iowa Baseball Museum of Norway, 2012.

Kerrane, Kevin. *Dollar Sign on the Muscle.* New York: Beaufort Books, 1984.

Lewis, Franklin. *The Cleveland Indians.* New York: Putnam, 1949.

Pluto, Terry. *Our Tribe: A Baseball Memoir.* New York: Simon & Schuster, 1999.

Ritter, Lawrence. *The Glory of Their Times.* New York: Macmillan, 1966.

Sarnoff, Gary. *The Wrecking Crew of '33: The Washington Senators' Last Pennant.* Jefferson, NC: McFarland, 2009.

Schneider, Russell. *The Cleveland Indians Encyclopedia.* 3d. ed. New York: Sports Publishing, 2005.

Seymour, Harold, and Dorothy Seymour Mills. *Baseball: The Golden Age.* New York: Oxford University Press, 1971.

Tattersall, John C. "Clarifying an Early Home Run Record." *Baseball Research Journal* 1 (1972).
Thorn, John, Pete Palmer and Michael Gersman, eds. *Total Baseball.* 7th ed. Kingston, NY: Total Sports Publishing, 2001.
Trumpold, Cliff. *Now Pitching: Bill Zuber from Amana.* Amana, IA: Lakeside Press, 1992.
Voigt, David Q. *From the Commissioners to Continental Expansion.* Vol. 2 of *American Baseball.* Norman: University of Oklahoma Press, 1970.
Wiley, George. *One Wall and 357 Doubles: The Story of the 1936 Cleveland Indians.* Cleveland: SABR, 1990.
Wolff, Miles, and W. Lloyd Johnson. *The Encyclopedia of Minor League Baseball.* 3d ed. Durham, NC: Baseball America, 2007.

Newspapers and Periodicals

Baseball Digest
Baseball Research Journal
Benton County Star
Benton County Star-Bulletin
Cedar Rapids Gazette
Cedar Rapids Republican
Cedar Valley Times
Chicago Sun-Times
Chicago Tribune
Cleveland Indians Media Guide, 2011
Cleveland News
Cleveland Plain Dealer
Cleveland Press
Des Moines Register
Life
Longview (TX) News-Journal
Look
Muscatine (IA) Journal
New York Times
New York World-Telegram
Nine: A Journal of Baseball History and Culture
Religious Herald, Virginia Baptist Weekly
Sport
The Sporting News
Sports Illustrated
Toledo News-Bee
Youngstown (OH) Vindicator

Interviews and Correspondence

Elden Auker, phone interview, January 14, 1995.
Mike Boddicker, phone interview, October 16, 2009.
Bob Feller, letter to author, dated July 27, 1994; phone interview, November 8, 1994.
Rick Ferrell, phone interview, June 11, 1994.
Denny Galehouse, letter to author, dated August 2, 1994.
Mel Harder, letter to author, received December 8, 1996; phone interview, December 8, 1996.
Ralph Hodgin, phone interview, September 20, 1994.
Willis Hudlin, phone interview, July 6, 1994.
Roy Hughes, letter to author, dated August 1, 1994.
Bruce Kimm, interview November 19, 2009.
Thornton Lee, letter to author, dated August 24, 1994.
Harold Primrose, interview, September 12, 2009.

Bibliography

Hal Trosky, Jr., interview, October 12, 2012.
James Trosky, email exchange and phone interview, July 14, 2015.
Lorraine Trosky, interview, August 15, 1996.
James Van Scoyoc, interview, November 4, 2009.
Susan Volz, interview, November 12, 2009.

Websites

Baseball-Reference.com.
Encyclopedia of Arkansas History and Culture, http://www.encyclopediaofarkansas.net.
Encyclopedia of Cleveland History, http://www.ech.case.edu.
Iowa Baseball Museum of Norway (IA), norwaybaseballmuseum.org/.
Iowa Baseball Project, http://www.chapters.sabr.org/fieldofdreams/iowa-baseball-project.
National Baseball Hall of Fame, Baseballhall.org.
Negro League Baseball eMuseum, Kansas State University College of Education, http://coe.k-state.edu/annex/nlbemuseum/nlbemuseum.html.
Negro Leagues Baseball Players Association, nlbpa.com/the-negro-league-teams/chicago-union giants.
Retrosheet, http://www.retrosheet.org.
SABR Baseball Biography Project, sabr.org/bioproject.
The Sprouting News, http://www.mlblogsthesproutingnews.wordpress.com/.

Index

Index